W9-CZA-542

WILD COAST

MARIANNE TAYLOR

WILD COAST

A celebration of the places where land meets sea

BLOOMSBURY
LONDON · NEW DELHI · NEW YORK · SYDNEY

For Alison. With fond memories of the seaside summers of our childhood...
and thank you for forgiving me over the beach-ball incident.

Bloomsbury Natural History
An imprint of Bloomsbury Publishing Plc

50 Bedford Square	1385 Broadway
London	New York
WC1B 3DP	NY 10018
UK	USA

www.bloomsbury.com
BLOOMSBURY and the Diana logo are trademarks of Bloomsbury Publishing Plc
First published 2015

© Marianne Taylor, 2015
© Photos Marianne Taylor 2015 except as noted on p.208

Marianne Taylor has asserted her right under the Copyright, Designs and Patents Act, 1988,
to be identified as Author of this work.

All rights reserved. No part of this publication may be reproduced or transmitted in any form
or by any means,electronic or mechanical, including photocopying, recording, or any information
storage or retrieval system,without prior permission in writing from the publishers.

No responsibility for loss caused to any individual or organisation acting on or refraining from action
as aresult of the material in this publication can be accepted by Bloomsbury or the author.

British Library Cataloguing-in-Publication Data

A catalogue record for this book is available from the British Library.

ISBN: PB: 978-1-4081-8178-2
ePDF: 978-1-4081-8640-4
ePub: 978-1-4081-8641-1

10 9 8 7 6 5 4 3 2 1

Designed by Nicola Liddiard, Nimbus Design
Printed in China

To find out more about our authors and books visit www.bloomsbury.com. Here you will find extracts,
author interviews, details of forthcoming events and the option to sign up for our newsletters.

Contents

Below Observing the daily life of Puffins, such as these on Skomer island, Pembrokeshire, is one of the great joys of coastal wildlife-watching.

Everyone who enjoys country walks and wildlife-watching will have noticed the special magic of the 'edge' – where one kind of habitat meets another. Meadows adjoining woodland, the uplands where forest gives way to open moor or heath, the reedy margin of a lake – all are places where wildlife seems particularly rich and abundant. The animals and plants typical of each habitat type are joined by others, adapted to the particular features of the edge in question, or adapted to move easily between the two contrasting habitat types. This effect is no more striking than along our coastline – the point where land meets sea.

Nowhere in the British Isles is more than 113 kilometres from the sea, and the ratio of coastline to land area is very high compared to similar-sized island

To measure a coastline

If you look at a very small-scale map of the world, the coastlines of Britain and Ireland (in fact of all coastlines) are necessarily simplified – it is not possible to capture all the ins and outs without moving to a larger scale. At an increased scale, more detail can be shown on a map. If you make a measurement of the coastline from a small-scale and a large-scale map, the result from the smaller scale version will be shorter. For example, if you measure the coastline of the island of Great Britain as a series of connecting straight lines, each 100km long, you'll get a total length of some 2,800km. If you reduce the lines' length to 50km, more detail can be covered and the total increases to 3,400km. Even the 50km scale is still vastly too coarse to capture any real detail. But to how large a scale would you have to go to obtain an accurate result?

This turns out be an almost impossible task. The complexity of the coastline increases a little more with every increment of scale. Even down to the centimetre, more detail is revealed. The coastline has similar properties to the mathematical phenomenon known as a fractal – a curve which changes in complexity according to measurement scale. Fractals are in theory infinite in length, and while coastlines are not true fractals, if our measurement of the British Isles' coastline starts to account for individual rocks and pebbles, we would (eventually) come up with a very large number indeed. The fact that the coastline shape constantly changes thanks to tidal action only makes things more confusing.

So anyone setting out to measure coastlines will need to choose a scale, and then at least different countries' coastlines can be compared accurately. In a mapping project using a 1:250,000 scale, the World Resources Institute gives the UK a coastline of 19,717km, and Ireland 6,437km. That places them at 16th and 38th place respectively among the 195 nations that the project assessed (of which 34 are landlocked). In terms of land area, the UK's and Ireland's positions are 80th and 120th respectively.

groups. Our coastline's course is, in many regions, akin to a highly challenging rally course, with sweeping chicanes one moment and tight hairpins the next, and with more than 1,000 smaller islands on top of the main land masses of Great Britain and Ireland, the total length of coastline is well over 20,000 kilometres – although differing methods of measurement makes it extremely difficult to assign a definitive value. Along this course, our coastal terrain changes from shingle to sand to cliff to mudflat to boulder-beach, each hosting its own distinct wildlife community. In some areas, the coastal flavour of the habitat reaches back inland many kilometres, along the banks of tidal rivers for example. With seaside towns, once you are off the beach and beyond the esplanade it can seem no different, from a wildlife point of view, to any inland town – but there are differences, if you know where to look for them.

The wilder parts of the British coastline harbour some very

special animals and plants, and their populations here are of global significance. For example, of the 25 species of seabirds that breed on our cliffs and beaches, 21 are here in internationally important numbers. While no seabirds breed only in the British Isles, we do have more than 93 per cent of the world's breeding Manx Shearwaters, and more than 50 per cent of the world's Gannets and Great Skuas. Some less noticeable coastal species are indeed unique or endemic to the British Isles, such as *Eudarcia richardsoni*, an exquisite little piebald moth found only on the Dorset coast, the beautiful Scottish primrose that flowers only on the north coast of Scotland, and the miniscule Ivell's Sea Anenome, known only from Widewater Lagoon in Sussex.

The coast also offers temporary lodgings for some of the world's great animal travellers, with hundreds of thousands of migrating waders stopping off at our estuaries on their migrations, and more than a quarter of the world's 96 species of whales, dolphins and

Nature reserves & protected areas

Most of the larger nature reserves in the UK are managed by the Royal Society for the Protection of Birds (RSPB) or by local Wildlife Trusts. Others are National Nature Reserves (NNRs), designated as such by the government's relevant body (in England, for example, NNRs are designated by Natural England), while local authorities designate and manage Local Nature Reserves (LNRs) The European Union also designates areas which should be protected for nature conservation – these are Special Protection Areas (SPAs) and Special Areas of Conservation (SACs). In Ireland, important areas for wildlife are designated Statutory Nature Reserves. An international designating body is the Ramsar Convention, which identifies wetland sites of particular conservation value (Ramsar sites).

Many important sites will hold several of these designations.

Besides land that is protected specifically to conserve the wildlife it harbours, many other stretches of wild coastline are guarded against excessive development simply because of their value as wonderful landscapes. These are Areas of Outstanding Natural Beauty or AONBs (a similar scheme designates National Scenic Areas in Scotland). Another designation which affords some protection from development is Site of Special Scientific Interest (SSSI); its equivalent in Northern Ireland is Area of Special Scientific Interest (ASSI). The nature of the scientific interest may be biological but also can related to interesting geology or physical geography.

Introduction

porpoises regularly visiting our inshore waters. Our islands lie across a point where cool polar waters collide with warm water brought our way via a current known as the North Atlantic drift, and they are also the first landfall for flying animals that are pushed across the Atlantic by the prevailing westerly winds. It is no surprise that a huge diversity of species has been recorded along British coasts.

The human population of Britain has an innate attachment to the coastline, with research indicating that most of us would much rather spend a day at the seaside than walking in the countryside, and in the UK five per cent of us live by the sea – that's three million people, many of them in coastal cities like Brighton, Portsmouth, Plymouth, Cardiff, Swansea, Liverpool, Newcastle, Belfast and Edinburgh. For the 57 million UK citizens who live inland, holidays by the seaside are enduringly popular, with dozens of sleepy coastal towns coming to life in summer as holidaymakers swarm in. Tourists may temporarily double or triple a seaside town's population, and their needs provide for hundreds or thousands of seasonal jobs. Coastal development to support

Above

Migrating Whimbrels and other Arctic-breeding waders will stop off at suitable coastlines anywhere in Britain.

the tourist trade has inevitably resulted in the destruction or deterioration of large tracts of formerly wildlife-rich habitat, although this pattern of loss shows huge variation from one end of Britain to the other.

Not all seaside tourism is bad news for wildlife. From many seaside towns you can book a boat tour in search of seabirds, cetaceans and other marine life – such trips are becoming increasingly popular in some areas, and of course they depend on the protection of the wildlife itself as well as coastal and marine habitats. Some coastal holiday-makers come in search of nothing but wildlife, and in many parts of the British Isles it is easy to fill a week based at a seaside town with visits to a succession of nearby coastal nature reserves.

VISITING THE COAST

Walking and looking for wildlife in coastal habitats is hugely rewarding and enjoyable, but in a few areas there are certain hazards to keep in mind. A modicum of planning and common sense is needed to ensure nothing happens to spoil your day.

Tides

Many beaches are not fully covered by the sea at even the highest tide and you can safely walk along them at any time without the risk of being cut off. If visiting an unfamiliar area, check first whether this is the case, and if not, use tide tables to make sure you will not be caught out. The BBC's website include tide tables for the UK – visit **www.bbc.co.uk/weather/ coast_and_sea/tide_tables**, and for Ireland the *Irish Times* publishes tide times here: **www. irishtimes.com/news/weather/ tides**. These guides show not just the times of high and low tide but tide heights, which can vary dramatically from day to day. The biggest high tides and lowest low tides ('spring' tides) occur on the new moon and full moon, when the Moon and Sun are aligned and the Earth experiences their combined gravitational pull. When the position of the Sun and Moon form a right angle with the earth, their two gravitational forces are opposed to each other and so partly cancel each other out. At these times the difference between high and low tide is much more modest; these are known as 'neap tides'.

Mudflats

Some soft muddy shores, exposed at low tide, are extremely hazardous to walk across and if you attempt to do so you could sink in and become stuck. Some of the most dangerous mudflats are often found at estuary mouths – warning signs may be present, but even if not it is best to avoid walking across even small river mouths. When walking on sandy beaches always take care and be prepared to turn back if things get very soft underfoot.

Left The British Isles is a world leader for marine mammal-watching, with great opportunities to see cetaceans such as Common Dolphins.

Above Visitors to Marazion, Cornwall, will want to visit the splendid St Michael's Mount, but this is also a great place to watch seabirds in winter.

Clifftops

The hazards of walking too near the cliff edge are obvious, but it is particularly important to take great care if walking on the tops of cliffs formed from soft rock, such as sandstone, which are prone to rockfalls. The chances of a rockfall are higher after prolonged wet weather. If walking with dogs be particularly careful, as some dogs are quite fearless and very easily distracted by interesting sights and smells.

Rocks

Exploring rockpools is one of the great joys of visiting the seaside. Where rocks are covered with seaweed or algae, they are likely to be very slippery underfoot, so always wear grippy boots or shoes, take great care or avoid such areas and stick to the edges of rocky outcrops. A fall onto barnacle-crusted rock can cause very nasty injuries.

Also keep in mind that lower-lying landward parts of rocky outcrops may become covered by seawater before higher rocks further out, as the tide comes in, so take care not to get cut off.

Weather

Because of the lack of natural shelter along most stretches of coastline, it's important to be

Below The Arctic Tern is perhaps the world's greatest animal traveller. It can be seen in northern Britain in summer but migrates more than 20,000 miles south for the winter.

Introduction

prepared for the weather conditions when heading for the seaside. On sunny days, even at cooler times of the year, you may need suncream and a hat, and windproof clothing will make a walk along an exposed coast more comfortable. Where storm surges are forecast, it is safest to avoid coastal areas altogether, as in these extreme conditions sea walls and other defences may be overtopped.

This book celebrates the wildlife and wildness of our coastlines, from town to countryside, from sweeping sandy beaches to sheer, high cliff edges, from rugged and rocky shores fending off angry seas to mellow and pastoral coastal grazing marshes.

Habitat by habitat, we look at the characteristics of the terrain, what makes it the way it is, and the particular wild animals and plants it supports, before picking out a selection of prime examples from the extent of Britain and Ireland's coast.

Of course, coastal habitats don't occur in isolation – they grade into each other to a greater or lesser extent. Shingle beaches often have patches of sand, and shingle may accumulate between dunes. Tiny sandy bays form in between rocky outcrops, and cliff-falls produce boulder beaches. Marshland is associated with estuary, and seaside towns often hold little patches of all kinds of wilder coastal habitats.

Many of the sites given here include a mix of habitat types, which only enhances their interest and appeal to wildlife.

Top The western coast of Britain has numerous beautiful, sheltered little sandy bays, such as Kynance.

Above Low tide provides a few precious hours to investigate the wonderful wildlife of the intertidal zone.

Sand

The sandy beach is loved far more by day-trippers and holiday-makers than the less barefoot-friendly shingle beach. On a hot day in August in south-east England, it's standing room only on the beaches at Camber Sands or West Wittering. Wildlife-watchers may have more luck visiting in winter, when the shoreline can teem with flocks of waders, all intent on extracting the myriad invertebrate creatures that live out their lives burrowed deep in the sand along the intertidal zone. Beyond the tide's reach, the dry sand is built up in the form of steep dunes, bound together with Marram Grass, and progressively the dunes become more fully vegetated as you head inland. This succession of habitats supports its own distinct set of ecosystems.

GROUND TO DUST

Sand is the product of erosion, by the action of the sea and wind on rock and also sea erosion on the hard remains of marine animals, such as the shells of molluscs. There is no difference in terms of composition between sand, silt and gravel, but geologists differentiate them by the size of the grains. Silt particles have a diameter of less than 0.0625mm, gravel particles a diameter of between 2 and 64mm. Sand particles are in between these two – a grain of sand is officially anything between 0.0625–2mm. The three grain sizes may be found mixed together, though similar-sized particles tend to be deposited along the same stretches of coastline through the sorting action of the sea.

Most sand on British beaches is composed of silica (silicon dioxide) in the form of quartz, but other forms of silica may also be found as sand particles, including flint and chert (in its various forms, silica is the most abundant mineral in the Earth's crust). The quartz sand that is the main constituent of sandy beaches in Britain has a golden or yellow colour when dry, and under very close examination the grains look like tiny, often translucent pebbles. Solid white particles among them are likely to be of animal origin – the smashed remains of mollusc shells, or even bone fragments.

SHELL-SEEKING

The sandy shoreline looks, at first glance, almost devoid of life. It is not, of course, but most of the small organisms that live in this habitat are buried well within the sand. On the surface, you may find their remains – the intertidal zone of a sand beach is often a good hunting ground for mollusc shells. We tend to use the term 'shellfish' to include both molluscs and crustaceans, especially when the discussion is

Above A close look at sand grains reveals a variety of colours and variable opacity.

Left Erosion of shells by wave action eventually produces a fine and very white sand.

Building a beach

The sea's action on the shore reshapes the coast over time – it erodes and carries material away, eating into the coastline, but it also deposits sediment of various kinds, to form beaches. Sea currents and the prevailing direction of the wind and waves relative to the orientation of the coastline determines what process happens where. The sedimentary material that forms beaches comes from various sources – some is washed down to the sea via rivers, some is lifted from the sea floor, and some comes from rocks and cliff bases eroded by wave action. Sandy beaches are more likely to form in sheltered spots, such as spaces between rocky outcrops, as in rougher seas sand tends to be held in suspension in fast-moving water, and only larger rocks and stones have the weight to settle out on the shore.

The waves that come ashore are of two kinds – constructive and destructive. The same beach can experience both kinds, with constructive waves more frequent in calmer seas than rough water, and more frequent on all beach types during summer. Constructive waves move sediment up the beach while destructive waves carry it back down towards the sea. Also at work on open stretches of coastline is longshore drift, the gradual movement of sediment in one direction. This process occurs because waves strike the beach at an angle, so pick up sediment on their way in, and then deposit it slightly further along on the backwash. These processes gradually reshape beaches, but events such as tsunamis, very high tides and storm surges cause dramatic changes over a far shorter time.

Wet sand exposed when the tide falls offers feeding ground for wading birds, gulls and, on the strandline, opportunists like corvids (including the rare Chough in parts of Wales, western Scotland and Ireland). Seaducks and terns may come ashore to rest on the sand just at the edge of the waves. The animals that actually live buried in the wet sand are not often seen but evidence of their presence may be noticed. In particular, the curly 'castings' of wet sand left by Lugworms can be extremely common on the wet sandy shore. The worms themselves, which resemble earthworms but with tiny 'legs' and can be more than 20cm long, live their whole lives in their U-shaped burrows. They ingest sand and extract particles of organic matter from it, excreting the rest as the 'casting'. This marks the 'tail end' of the worm's burrow, and if you look around it you may see a depression in the sand nearby that indicates the 'head end' of the same worm's burrow.

The sand carried highest up the beach, at high tide, has the longest time to dry out, and once dry it can be moved further up the beach by onshore winds, carried in a rolling motion along the ground. The result is sand that is never (or almost never) reached by the sea, which forms dunes. A range of plant species, most notably marram grass, can grow on dunes and help to 'fix' the hills of sand in place, resulting in a stable structure that provides a barrier, protecting the ground further inland from tidal and storm surges. Continuing to move further from the sea, the ground becomes increasingly stable and more firmly anchored by an increasing variety of plant types, as the loose 'yellow dunes' transition to fixed and fully vegetated 'grey dunes'.

Left In many areas, numerous lugworm casts decorate the intertidal parts of sandy beaches.

Sand

Right Living mussels often carry passengers in the form of Acorn Barnacles, though the barnacles attached to rock may survive longer.

of gastronomy rather than zoology. But the 'sea shells' we find on the beach are the remains of molluscs.

The molluscs make up the taxonomic phylum Mollusca. To put that into context, the phylum to which we humans belong is Chordata, the grouping that includes all vertebrate organisms. There are some 85,000 species of molluscs, and they make up 23 per cent of described marine animals – they are better represented in sealife than any other phylum. The group is divided into about 10 taxonomic classes, of which two – Gastropoda and Bivalvia –

account for the various common seashells we find washed up on our sandy beaches.

Gastropod molluscs have a single shell, often with a coiled, spiral shape. The familiar Garden Snail is a classic example, as well as one of the relatively small number of molluscs to live on land. Bivalve molluscs, as their name suggests, have rather simpler paired shells or 'valves', which are fixed to each other with a small hinge, and can open or close. Often the hinge is broken after the animal itself dies, and the shells are then found as separated halves.

Many bivalves, such as mussels, live fixed to rock or other substrates, sometimes in the intertidal zone as they can shut their shells when exposed to the air and thus protect themselves from drying out. When covered by water again, their shells open, and seawater flows in. The animals can then extract nutrients, sucking seawater in and squirting it out again via a pair of siphons, and filtering out tiny planktonic organisms and other fragments of organic material. Others, including cockles, live burrowed deep into sand or mud, and still others, for example scallops, can swim freely from place to place, using their siphons to 'jet-propel' themselves through the water.

Gastropods tend to live on rocky or other solid substrates. Some move freely around across the surface when covered by water, and are very like snails in their movement. Others are much less mobile. We tend to think of limpets, for example, as completely fixed to the spot, as they 'stick' so strongly to the spot and the edge of their shell wears a groove into the rock, but when underwater they do move short distances to find food, returning to their 'home scar' to lock down before they are exposed to the air. Most gastropods have a rasping, toothed and ribbonlike 'tongue' called a radula, which they use in various ways to feed. Limpets scrape algae from rock surfaces, while predatory whelks use their radulas to bore holes in the shells of other molluscs.

Molluscs can be incredibly long-lived. The Ocean Quahog, a large species of deep-sea clam, has been shown to be capable of living for more than 500 years – these animals can be reliably aged because their shells bear annual growth rings. However, when a mollusc dies, its soft body quickly decays (if not eaten by a predator) and its shell may then be carried long distances by the sea before finally washing up ashore. Of course, most of the shells we find on beaches are from molluscs that died not far away, but occasionally rarities from thousands of miles away are found on British shores, especially after severe weather events. The strandline will hold the highest numbers of washed-up shells, but on many sandy shores there is a good distribution of shells throughout the intertidal zone.

TYPES OF SEASHELLS
The following mollusc species are among the most frequent finds on sandy shorelines.

BIVALVES
Banded Wedge Shell (*Donux vittatus*) This small and pretty bivalve is a common find on sandy beaches, usually discovered as disarticulated single valves lying open side down on wet sand. The upperside of the valve is smooth and shiny, and variable in colour, ranging from yellow or golden through pinkish-white with darker bands.

The inside of the shell is also glossy and usually pinkish. The shape is a simple oval wedge, the hinge set towards the more pointed end of the shell. Banded Wedge Shells live buried in sand or mud and shells found in good condition on the sand surface are probably of very local origin, as they are too delicate to survive long in the sea.

Razor Clam or Razorshell (*Ensis ensis*) Another sand-burrowing bivalve, this mollusc's rectangular shell is highly distinctive, being much longer than it is wide, with parallel edges and very square corners. The outer surface is glossy and usually a rather dull greenish-brown colour, with prominent growth rings. This shell can be

Below After a stormy spell, Razor Clam shells are sometimes washed up in huge numbers.

Right Scallop shells are very attractive, though not very robust so those found on beaches are often damaged.

Below Cockle shells are common beachcombing finds, usually disarticulated from their 'other halves'.

extremely abundant in the tideline.

Common Cockle (*Cerastoderma edule*) One of the most recognisable shell types, the half-sphere valve of the Common Cockle bears distinctive ridges running perpendicular to its concentric growth rings. It is a sturdy and solid shell, less likely to be damaged by the sea's action than more fragile bivalves. When alive, Common Cockles live buried in soft substrate, and use their siphons to draw in sea water from which they filter out nutrients.

Great Scallop (*Pecten maximus*) This often large mollusc has a superficially cockle-like shell, with a round shape and strong ridges, but it is flattened rather than hemispherical, giving it the look of a fan. It also has a smaller, flat-edged fan-shape at its hinge, although these pieces frequently get damaged or break off entirely. The outer side of the shell is usually a warm red-brown colour. Scallops are free-living molluscs and can swim with ease by rapidly opening and closing its valves.

Thin Tellin (*Angulus tenuis*) Rather similar to the Banded Wedge Shell, this common species has a more rounded shell shape and is a little smaller. It also lacks the strong gloss of the Banded Wedge Shell. It is an attractively marked and coloured species, with prominent growth rings in various shades of pink. It lives at a shallow depth in the substrate and extends its siphon above the sand into the water. Fish may nibble the siphon tips but the mollusc is able to regrow them if they are damaged.

Common or Blue Mussel *(Mytulis edulis)* This very common and familiar bivalve is the best known and most abundant mussel species around our coasts. It is important commercially as well as being a key food source for many marine animals, including eiders, scoters and other seaducks. It forms dense colonies (mussel beds) on substrates, including some that are exposed at low tide as well as in deeper water. The shell is elongated and tapers to a point at one end. Its outer surface has a rough texture and a blackish-blue colour, often with silvery markings, and may carry living or dead barnacles.

GASTROPODS
Common Whelk *(Bucinnum undatum)* A large gastropod with a whortled, pointed shell, the Common Whelk is abundant around our coasts and is harvested for food in some areas. The light reddish or grey-brown shell is rather delicate and it is rare to find one completely intact. Sometimes the outer layers are missing entirely and only the more solid central spiral remains. Common Whelks live mainly on soft substrate and prey on other small marine animals. They attack other shelled molluscs by boring holes through their shells. Empty Common Whelk egg-cases resemble clusters of little polystyrene balls, and are

Below The largest gastropod shell you're likely to find on a British beach is the Common Whelk.

frequently found in the strandline.

Netted Dog Whelk *(Nassarius reticulatus)* This species has a similar shell shape to the Common Whelk but is much smaller. The shell is strongly ridged with cross-bands, giving rise to the 'netted' texture. The shell is usually brown or pinkish and is quite solid and robust, meaning it is often found intact or with just the tip of the spire missing. Unlike the Common Whelk, the Netted Dog Whelk feeds on dead and decaying organic matter, and can travel rapidly between food sources.

Needle Whelk *(Bittium reticulatum)* Much taller than it is wide, this attractive shell is found primarily on southern and western coasts. It has a rough surface and a gently tapered shape, with obvious whorls, and a grey-brown colour. The living mollusc feeds on sponges.

Common Limpet *(Patella vulgata)* Because many Common Limpets live on rocks and artificial structures in the intertidal zone, they are encountered alive as often, if not more often, than their empty shells are found on the beach. The shell is a simple pointed cap shape, with ridges radiating from the centre, though in detached empty shells these ridges quickly wear away, leaving a smooth surface. This shape, with the opening the widest point of the shell, allows the limpet to fix itself very strongly to its

Right A well-weathered but still recognisable Common Limpet shell on the strandline.

Opposite Sandy beaches aren't just for summer. Beachcombing is often particularly rewarding the day after an autumn or winter storm.

'perch', so it remains airtight when exposed at low tide, and is a difficult challenge for predators. When covered by water it moves slowly across the rock, browsing on algae, before returning to its 'home scar' for the low tide period.

Slipper Limpet (*Crepidula fornicata*) This mollusc was accidentally introduced to Europe from the western Atlantic in the 20th century, and has spread to much of the coastline of England and Wales. It is considered to be an invasive species, able to outcompete other molluscs for space and food. It is oval and smooth, slightly curved, and mottled brown in colour. On the underside there is a 'flap' of shell covering half of its opening, giving it the appearance of a round-bottomed shoe or a boat with a 'half deck'. This flap of shell is more hard-wearing than the outer layer and is often found in isolation, a small, flattened but quite chunky white slab of shell. Slipper Limpets live on rocks, and also on top of clusters of other rock-dwelling molluscs and form stacking towers, those in the upper layers mating with the ones below.

Flat Periwinkle (*Litterina obtusata*) One of several periwinkle species that live around our coasts, this pretty mollusc is shaped like many of our familiar land snail species, with a round whorled shell that has no pointed spire. Its shell colour is highly variable, and may be yellow, red-brown, black, greenish or brown – usually plain but occasionally with striped markings. Living Flat Periwinkles may be found on intertidal rocks, and their empty shells on beaches are sometimes found in large numbers.

Arctic Cowrie (*Trivia arctica*) Large cowries of various species from tropical shores are familiar as ornamental objects, with their glossy, boldly patterned shells. The Arctic Cowrie is a small, plain, white species, with a rough and lightly ridged shell, but has

Right A cluster of colourful Flat Periwinkle shells.

Far right Upside-down, a Slipper Limpet shell reveals the shape that gives it its name.

Sand

the familiar egg shape with a long, slit-shaped opening. It is most likely to be found on beachs in the north. It lives below the intertidal zone, and feeds exclusively on sea squirts.

TIDE-RUNNER

Various wading birds make use of sandy shores, but most prefer softer, muddier ground. The one wader that is most likely to turn up on sandy beaches is, appropriately enough, the Sanderling. A charming, very small and dumpy wader, it draws

Left Although they seem scared of getting their toes wet when feeding, Sanderlings will wade into the shallows to bathe.

Below Two of these Sanderlings are marked with coloured leg rings and flags as part of a research project.

Top In winter plumage, Sanderlings are the whitest small shorebirds you'll see in Britain. This group is foraging with two Dunlins and a Turnstone.

Above Sanderlings use their bills to probe as well as snap up prey, as this one's sand-encrusted bill illustrates.

attention through its habit of rushing back and forth by the shoreline, close to the breaking wavelets, as if playing 'chicken' with the water. They are most familiar to British birdwatchers as winter visitors, when they have almost pure white plumage. Any time you take a walk along a sizeable sandy beach in winter, you are likely to encounter Sanderlings in small flocks, running like clockwork toys along the wave edge, or roosting higher up the beach.

The prey types favoured by these birds are very small marine isopods (woodlouse-like crustaceans) and crabs, both of which live in the sand close to

the waveline, and may surface briefly when the wash of a wave covers them. The Sanderlings run along in a pack, frequently probing the sand at the water's edge, and by this ad hoc method they sometimes strike lucky and catch an isopod or crab that didn't re-bury itself fast enough. They will also forage further up the beach, and may pick at carrion as well as chase and catch flies and other insects. Every so often the whole flock walks into the shallow water to bathe, or clusters for 10-minute power-nap just beyond the reach of the water.

In winter, Sanderlings may be found on suitable beaches

Sand

Left Like other shorebirds, Sanderlings' sleep patterns are influenced by the tide, and they often take daytime 'cat-naps'.

practically anywhere in the world, but they breed in the high Arctic, across North America as well as Eurasia. They nest on the tundra, well above the treeline and often well inland. Once a female Sanderling has laid her clutch of eggs, she quite often leaves her mate in charge of incubation and rearing the young, while she forms a new pair bond with a different male (if she can find one who isn't already tied up with parental responsibilities), and produces a second clutch of eggs. This breeding system, known as serial polyandry, gives females a much improved chance of producing at least some

offspring during the brief and capricious Arctic summer. The chicks are able to run from danger and feed themselves from an hour or two after hatching, so only one parent is needed to take care of them.

In spring, Sanderlings may not set off for their breeding grounds until May, and those whose nests fail will be making their way back south as early as June. Additionally, each year a few birds won't attempt to breed at all, so in fact it is possible to see Sanderlings around our coasts all year round, especially in the north, though there are far more here in winter than at other times. Most waders are quite

nervous and flighty but Sanderlings tend to be quite approachable. If you sit on the beach near a feeding flock, and keep still and quiet, they may well wander very close, too absorbed in their search for food to concern themselves with your presence.

Winter-plumaged Sanderlings are mostly white but with a blackish patch at the bend of their wings, and light grey crowns and upperparts. They have black legs and almost straight black bills that are rather stout for a wader. They also have only three toes on each foot, not four like most waders. The hind toe is missing – which may facilitate the bird's distinctive rapid running style. In breeding plumage, they are much more colourful than usual, sporting rich ginger-red heads and breasts, though the extent of the coloration is very variable, and within a small flock of summer-plumaged birds, no two will look exactly alike.

Although Sanderlings like to associate with other Sanderlings, their gatherings also often attract one or two other small waders, especially Dunlins and Ringed Plovers. By the same token, large flocks of Turnstones and Purple Sandpipers gathered together on rocky or shingle coasts may attract the odd stray Sanderling.

Below Thick stands of Marram Grass offer safe places for flocks of Starlings to rest in between their foraging forays.

DUNES

In the world's great sand deserts, where low rainfall prevents colonisation by plants, the wind constantly builds, sculpts and reshapes the dry sand into spectacular towering steep-faced dunes. But the dunes that form behind our sandy beaches have a more stable structure, thanks to the pioneering plants that are able to survive in this tough environment.

Marram Grass is a tall, coarse, tussock-forming grass, which has what it takes to survive and thrive on sand dunes. The root system spreads downwards and outwards from thick, tough rhizomes which anchor it solidly into the loose ground, and which can tolerate being immersed in salt water. Broken sections of rhizomes can resprout in new locations if carried away by the sea. The leaves have a waxy coating which protects them from sand thrown at them by the wind. The dense tussocks offer shelter for animals. Another important dune-stabilising grass is the smaller Sand Couch, which is also deep-rooted, and unlike Marram Grass requires contact with salty water to survive. Where these grasses grow, the dunes are somewhat stabilised but there is still movement of loose sand, and the ground is highly vulnerable to erosion.

incubation chambers for the eggs through June and July. Rare but increasing, thanks to strict conservation efforts, full legal protection, and reintroduction projects, Sand Lizards occur at just a few sites in Britain, on dunes adjoining coastal heath, as well as sandy heaths inland.

Another uncommon British animal with a liking for dunes is the Grayling butterfly. One of the 'browns', this is a large but rather drab species, and when settled with its wings closed and the forewings tucked under the silver-spangled hindwing, it has superlative camouflage against a background of sandy earth. It also has the habit of leaning its body over, to control how much of

Left The male Sand Lizard in his spring finery is a stunning little reptile.

Below At rest, a Grayling butterfly is perfectly camouflaged against a sandy and stony backdrop.

Sometimes where an area of dune vegetation is damaged or lost, perhaps through Rabbit burrowing activity, strong winds create a crater or 'blow-out' of open sand, which will then gradually be recolonised by dune plants.

Animals that live in dune systems include what is arguably Britain's most spectacular native reptile, the Sand Lizard. A much larger and more robust creature than the more familiar Common Lizard, the Sand Lizard is a beautiful animal, with an intricately patterned body and (in some breeding males) a dazzling vivid green base colour. Unlike the Common Lizard, which bears live young, Sand Lizards are egg-layers and the females dig burrows in the sand to serve as

Waves are most likely to deposit sand in bays, inlets and other sheltered places on the coastline.

its wing surface is exposed to the sun and thus regulate its body temperature (although it was formerly thought that this leaning behaviour was a way of further improving its camouflage, by reducing the size of its shadow).

Relatively few birds nest in the looser sand dunes, but those that do include Meadow Pipits and Ringed Plovers, the former nesting within grassy tussocks, and the latter in more open settings, relying on the resemblance of its eggs to pebbles – this species does also nest on pebble beaches. Some species of terns nest in colonies on the upper slopes of sandy beaches, but only in areas where the beaches are undisturbed by human activity through the summer. At some sites, lack of disturbance is ensured by fencing off the areas used by the terns, but they are extremely sensitive to disturbance and even if all seems to be going well it is not unusual for whole colonies to abandon a site if they feel unsafe. In stable dunes, Rabbits can establish warrens, and Shelducks will use Rabbit burrows as nest holes.

Where dunes are long-established and there is little or no regular sand movement, other plants can replace the grasses and vegetation cover can become complete. Scrubby plants such as Sea Buckthorn and Juniper provide cover for nesting birds, and shelter for

Right The distinctive Fen Orchid is a characteristic flower of dune slacks.

Far right Ringed Plovers will nest on undisturbed sandy beaches, as well as more stony shores.

migrants making landfall. In between the drier high ridges, dune 'slacks' can form. These low areas are naturally much damper than the high ground and a different range of plants colonises them, including in some areas rarities like the Fen Orchid. Another special type of dune vegetation is machair, which forms where the sand has a high proportion of shell fragments, resulting in a calcium-rich earth that supports particularly rich grassland. Machair is found in northern and western Scotland and western Ireland – and nowhere else in the world. It provides valuable grazing for livestock, and habitat for a range of wildlife including the Corncrake.

EXPLOITING THE UNDERCLIFF

Erosion of the seaward faces of long-established dunes can produce an exposed and relatively solid vertical undercliff. This material is soft enough for Sand Martins to dig their nesting burrows in it, and watching these busy birds going about their daily business of hunting, squabbling and rearing their young is a very pleasant way to pass a summer afternoon at the seaside.

Sand Martins look ill-equipped for heavy digging work, with their small feet and bills. Members of the swallow family, they are long-winged small birds with streamlined bodies, adapted for fast, agile and almost tireless flight in pursuit of winged insects. Many Sand Martin colonies are inland, in river banks, the sides of reservoirs, road and rail embankments and old quarries. At some nature reserves, colonies have become established at artificial concrete nesting walls into which suitable tunnels are pre-made. In natural sites like undercliffs, the martins have to do the work themselves, both members of the pair digging out a tunnel up to 120cm long. They use both bill and feet to dig, kicking loose material out behind them as they go. At the end of the tunnel they carve out an enlarged chamber for the actual nest, which they line with soft material such as grasses and feathers.

If you visit a Sand Martin colony in April, you'll see many birds coming into their nests carrying big fluffy feathers, which they have 'caught' on the wing. They will also land on the

Below Coastal undercliffs can provide ideal conditions for a Sand Martin colony to set up home.

Dunes and their vegetation are vulnerable to erosion, so visitors should stick to established paths across them wherever possible.

Right A Sand Martin on its way back to its burrow, with a bill-full of flies for its chicks.

Below Camber Sands is full of sun-seekers in summer, but a winter walk (or ride) can be wonderfully rewarding for wildlife-watching.

ground to pull up grasses. A month on and the birds will be bringing insect prey for their chicks, working from dawn until dusk. It is common for them to begin a second brood once the first has fledged, perhaps with a different mate and in a different burrow. Adults and youngsters alike begin their southwards migration in August, flying to sub-Saharan Africa for the winter.

The nesting colonies are rather vulnerable. Erosion from wind and heavy rain may cause the burrows to collapse, and storm surges could flood them out. Foxes and other predators will dig out the burrows if they are within reach (and they often are), while other predators like Sparrowhawks and even Grey Herons may lurk near the burrows to try to grab the adults as they arrive or depart. Sand Martins cope with these risks through a high reproductive rate, and by being very quick to set up new colonies when suitable new habitat becomes available. The Sand Martin has declined through the 20th century (probably because of droughts on its wintering grounds) and is currently amber-listed as a species of conservation concern, but its numbers are now slowly increasing.

PLACES TO VISIT

Here is a selection of the best sandy beaches and dune systems to watch wildlife around the British Isles.

ENGLAND

Camber Sands, East Sussex This extensive dune system in the south-west corner of East Sussex is hugely popular with holiday-makers and day-trippers in summer, but out of season the huge expanse of sand exposed at low tide can teem with waders, while the large and growing dune system – up to 1km wide – falls partly within an SSSI and is home to a range of rare animals and plants. Rare moths such as the Shore Wainscot occur here, and in winter Shore Larks and Snow Buntings sometimes turn up to forage along the strandline and in the dunes. In summer, Sandwich Terns can be seen feeding offshore. Camber Sands lies in between Rye Harbour Nature Reserve and RSPB Dungeness, two other coastal sites of huge wildlife value.

Braunton Burrows, Devon
England's largest dune system, measuring about 6km by 1.5km, this area on the north Devon coast is particularly important for its rich and diverse plant communities. The Burrows have many conservation designations – part of the area is a National Nature Reserve, it is also an SSSI and a Ramsar Site, and it forms the centre of the North Devon UNESCO Biosphere Reserve. Its habitats include the full range of successional vegetation communities that exist in dune systems, and as well as more than 400 plant species, it is home to rare invertebrates like the Amber Sandbowl Snail, and the Grayling butterfly.

Sefton coast, Merseyside The coastline between Crosby and Southport comprises two dozen kilometres of sandy beach and dune, several of which are protected as nature reserves. One of the largest is Ainsdale Sand Dunes National Nature Reserve. This coastline is home to the Sand Lizard and also to the rare Natterjack Toad, which uses shallow and warm temporary pools in dune slacks to spawn. In pockets of pine woodland adjoining the dunes, Red Squirrels have one of their few remaining English outposts. Some of the 1,000 or so wild plants in the area include beautiful rarities like the Dune Helleborine and Seaside Centaury. In summer, terns hunt along the coastline, and many waders feed and roost here in winter.

Above **A group of Common Gulls loaf on the edge of a bay in Ardnamurchan, west Scotland.**

Below Paddling in the shallows while looking out for interesting shells and stones is one of the great joys of visiting a sandy beach.

Opposite Dunes and acres of sandy beach at Holkham in north Norfolk.

Holkham, Norfolk The entire north Norfolk coast has a legendary status as a wildlife mecca, and the dunes and beach at Holkham are no exception. The extensive and picturesque dunes here have formed on top of old shingle ridges, some of the most impressively steep 'dune islands' only starting to develop as recently as the mid 20th century. The upper parts of the beach are home to nesting Little Terns, and fencing is used to keep their nests safe from the many tourists that visit this glorious area. Other breeding birds include Oystercatchers and Ringed Plovers. A remarkable and very rare insect has taken up residence here in recent years. The Antlion, a large lacewing-like creature with broad, patterned wings, spends its larval stages living buried in loose sand, at the bottom of a funnel-shaped 'pitfall' trap, waiting to catch and eat any other insect that falls down into the pit. Further along the coast, the sandy beach at Titchwell is part of the RSPB reserve, and holds impressive flocks of Sanderlings and other waders in winter.

Seahouses to Lindisfarne, Northumberland Wildlife-watchers visiting this area are probably here to visit the Farne Islands with their famous seabird colonies. The islands are reached by boat trips out of Seahouses. However, it is well worth exploring the coastline north of Seahouses as well. A walk along the shore in summer will bring sightings of some of the Farnes seabirds, with Sandwich Terns in particular coming very close to the land and perhaps resting on the beach, alongside Common Eiders which breed here, and will be guarding their ducklings in sheltered inlets from June. Sand Martins nesting in the undercliff are joined by Swifts that breed on the

promenade buildings. In winter, other seaducks join the Eiders, and flocks of waders gather on the shore, especially on the mudflats around Lindisfarne.

WALES

Freshwater West, Pembrokeshire
Freshwater West beach is a long west-facing sand beach, famous for its consistent and impressive surf. It plays host to international surfing tournaments and is a great place to watch this spectacular sport at all times of year. The beach and dunes beyond are also wildlife-rich, and a good place to see one of Wales' special birds, the Chough, which feeds in coastal fields and sometimes on the dunes. Otters can also be seen here, travelling between beach and land via a stream to the shore. Very low tides expose the remains of a petrified forest, while inland the dune slacks flush purple with a fine show of Southern Marsh and Pyramidal Orchids in summer.

Ynyslas, Ceredigion/Gwynned
Part of the Dyfi National Nature Reserve, this beach and dune system is extensive and still growing at a rapid rate. It is another site that has impressive numbers of orchids, including Marsh Helleborine, Northern Marsh and Bee Orchid, and the Sand Lizard was reintroduced here in 2009. Several scarce invertebrates here include the spider *Agroeca dentigera*, not known from any other British site, and the Welsh Vernal Mining Bee. Birds nesting in the dunes include important numbers of Ringed Plovers, and the site is also one of the best in Britain for records of the Kentish Plover, a sandy-beach specialist which formerly bred in Britain and may in due course recolonise.

Top right Big waves breaking off Sennen Cove in west Cornwall.

Above From Pembrokeshire beaches, you stand a chance of seeing the rare, distinctive and handsome Chough.

Polecats are among the mammals that may, with luck, be seen in the duneland. The National Nature Reserve rewards further exploration, with other habitats such as saltmarsh and estuarine raised bog, each with their own range of unusual wildlife.

SCOTLAND

Culbin Sands, Moray The beautiful beach at Culbin graduates into pine forest growing on the old dunes, giving a unique combination of habitat types. The trees are of non-natural origin, being planted on the dunes to protect Findhorn village from blowing sand, but have become home to a range of wildlife including the Crested Tit, one of Scotland's most iconic birds.

This dune system is Britain's largest, and some of its peaks are more than 30 metres high. Erosion is constantly reshaping the edge of the dunes, and the area must be managed actively so that trees which are about to be toppled are removed before they can be carried away by the sea. East of Culbin Forest is Findhorn Bay, a great spot to watch Ospreys fishing in the summer.

 The pretty Harebell is a common duneland flower.

Right Where pine forest meets duneland at Culbin Sands, you may find the charming Crested Tit.

Sand

Calgary Bay, Isle of Mull There are not many beaches around Britain that afford a good chance of seeing an eagle, but this stunning white-sand beach on the west side of Mull is one of them. The sand contains a high proportion of shell fragments, giving it its white colour, and it is backed by calcerous machair grassland. As well as Golden and White-tailed Eagles overflying the bay, this beach is regularly visited by foraging Otters, and there are nesting Sand Martins. A fine show of duneland flowers can be enjoyed through the summer, including species such as Harebell, Fairy Flax and Wild Pansy.

Redpoint, Highland At the end of the single-track B8056 is the little hamlet of Redpoint, just north of a small west-facing headland (Red Point). On either side of this headland are beautiful sandy beaches which, if they were in southern England, would be swarming with tourists on any sunny day, but because of their remote location (some 20km from the nearest sizeable village, Gairloch) they are quiet even in high summer, particularly the southern beach which is a 1km walk across rough ground from the nearest parking point. The beauty of the red sand beaches and the wonderful views across to Skye make the journey well worthwhile. The grassland behind the dunes is home to nesting Great Skuas, and the beaches themselves attract flocks of shorebirds all year round, making this a great spot to see species like Sanderlings and Dunlins in breeding

Top The extensive grassy dune system at Calgary Bay on the Isle of Mull, Scotland.

Above The high ground behind the Redpoint beaches is home to breeding Great Skuas.

plumage. Offshore you could see Minke Whales.

IRELAND

Whiterocks beach, Co Antrim

This lovely beach is backed by soft limestone cliffs, up to 228m high, which have been sculpted by erosion to form dramatic stacks, arches and caves. Nearby is the famous Giant's Causeway – it and Whiterocks beach falls within Northern Ireland's only World Heritaage site and are also part of a Special Area of Conservation. Whiterocks beach itself is an ASSI (Area of Special Scientific Interest). At its western end it merges into East Strand beach, which has a rich dune system. Seabirds and seals can be seen from the beach, and unusual finds on the tideline have included Buoy Barnacles, rare in Britain, which travel long distances by fixing themselves to floating objects in the sea.

Magherawarden, Co Donegal

Voted the second most beautiful beach in the world by readers of *The Observer* newspaper, this stunning mile-long beach of white sand is backed by gently sloping dunes. Beyond the dunes is machair grassland and then blanket bog with a rich variety of plant species. It is part of the Donegal Coast Special Protection Area, and is of national importance for its Choughs, which nest on cliffs nearby and forage on the dunes and machair.

Ballyteige Burrows, Co Wexford

An impressive vegetated dune system dominates this important wildlife site, designated an SAC and protected as a nature reserve. The grey dune area includes areas of acid heathland, increasing the plant diversity, and there are 'cobble valleys' in between the larger dunes, holding a shingle-type plant community with species like Yellow Horned Poppy. Many nationally rare invertebrates occur, and the area is important for nesting Little Terns, and visiting wildfowl and waders.

Below
A natural limestone arch on the beach at Magherawarden.

Sand

A Herring Gull drops a whelk from a great height onto a compacted sand foreshore, to break its shell.

Shingle

Shingle beaches will never have as much appeal as sandy ones for people who want to stretch out on a towel and sunbathe. For wildlife-watchers, too, they seem to have less to offer than sandy or rocky shores, but they hold their own special range of species, particularly on the higher slopes above the high water mark, where the stones are not subjected to constant rearrangement by the sea, and a shingle vegetation community can develop. Although 30 per cent of the UK coastline has shingle beaches, most are too narrow and not stable enough for any significant vegetation growth. On an international level, shingle beaches are uncommon, with the UK, Japan and New Zealand holding the lion's share.

STONY GROUND

The stones that form shingle beaches can resist being moved much by even quite rough seas, so shingle beaches tend to form on more exposed shores. They are still susceptible to the effects of longshore drift, and, left to their own devices some parts of the beach will shrink and others will grow according to prevailing onshore winds.

A close look at a typical shingle beach reveals pebbles of a variety of colours, sizes and shapes. The sea tends to wear them into smooth oval shapes, but those made from very hard rock such as flint are more likely to retain an irregular shape for longer. Sedimentary rocks like shale form flat pebble shapes in accordance with their layers.

The same individual pebble can be formed of two or more rock types, and while most pebbles are of natural origin a few started out as man-made materials. It is not unusual to find soft red brick pebbles, smooth dappled lumps of grey concrete, or small green or translucent stones that are seaworn pieces of broken glass. Occasionally, pebbles wholly or partly composed of semi-precious stones are found on British beaches.

Pebbles composed of soft rock will be worn away very quickly by the sea. You are unlikely to find chalk pebbles anywhere apart from at the base of a chalk cliff. Hard chert and flint stones though will survive for hundreds of years, though if they lie within the intertidal zone they will gradually wear to smaller and smaller sizes through sea erosion. Shingle beaches within the intertidal zone show a graduation in pebble sizes, with the biggest stones highest up the beach and on the steepest slopes. Shingle beaches tend to be much steeper than sandy beaches.

Below

A much-visited shingle beach is reshaped by human footfalls many times every day.

A SEASIDE OPPORTUNIST

It is difficult for small animals to survive among the pebbles of the intertidal zone, as the stones are constantly moved around and smashed against each other. This means that wading birds of nearly all species are much less likely to be found foraging on shingly shores compared to smoother sandy or silty beaches. There is one notable exception to this however.

The Turnstone is a very distinctive small to medium-sized wading bird, with bright orange legs and, in the breeding season, a gorgeous plumage pattern of black, white and reddish-chestnut, like a calico cat. This pattern blends surprisingly well against a variegated shingle beach. In winter it is drabber, the black and chestnut replaced with dark grey-brown, but still an attractive-looking bird with a portly frame, strikingly steep forehead and a shortish, strong bill that looks slightly uptilted. It can be found on all kinds of beaches but particularly on rocky and shingle shores.

This bird's foraging method is as its name suggests. It turns over loose bits of substrate, including stones but also washed-up clumps of seaweed and litter, in search of edible items below. On shingle beaches in particular, its finds tend to be half-crushed crabs or molluscs, or bits of washed-up carrion, as well as tiny fish and insects. It is gregarious at all times, going around in threes, fours or flocks of a few dozen or more, and there is much bickering among the group and sometimes scraps break out over ownership of a particularly tempting morsel of food.

Turnstones are adaptable birds, and in seaside towns will leave the beaches to look for dropped chips on the promenade, or dig worms out of ornamental seaside gardens. They will hang around fishing boats with the gulls in hope of thrown-away fish bits, and one unfortunate walker in Wales disturbed a Turnstone flock that were dining on a washed-up human corpse! Their flocks sometimes attract other waders, such as Sanderlings and especially Purple Sandpipers, but this is more likely on rocky shores rather than shingle beaches.

STRANDLINE STUDIES

When you walk along beaches at any time other than high tide, you will probably notice the strandline – an uneven band of seaweed and other debris

Left A Turnstone works its way along a seaweed-rich shingle strandline, in search of anything it can catch.

Below Constantly shifted by waves, shingle in the intertidal zone offers few opportunities for life to take root.

Right Common Whelk egg-cases are easily found in the strandline.

Below Seaweed, especially more robust brown and red species, is the main constituent of the strandline in most areas.

marking the high water mark. These objects are left behind as the waveline retreats, and both shingle and sandy beaches show strandlines. When walking along a beach it can be worthwhile sticking close to the strandline as you may make some interesting finds – although perhaps not too close, as strandlines – also known as tidelines – can be very smelly.

The seaweed that makes up the strandline will give you a snapshot of which species predominate locally, though more delicate seaweeds will be broken up by wave action and so won't be obvious in strandlines. On southern English beaches, much of the washed-up seaweed is Bladderwrack, which is tough enough to survive a battering, while in more westerly and northerly areas, the thick ribbon-like leaves of kelp can form the bulk of the strandline.

As well as marine plants, sea creatures are also washed up. The strandline often holds high numbers of mollusc shells, particularly larger species like Razor Clams, and the chalky white internal shells of cuttlefish. These 'cuttle-bones' are oval with flattened edges, thicker in the middle, and are still collected and used as a calcium source for caged birds like Budgerigars. The strandline also holds crab carapaces and often intact dead fish, as well as the empty egg-cases of Common Whelks and dogfish. The former are whitish clusters of polystyrene-like material, while the latter are squarish 'purses' with long filaments at each corner. Sometimes you will find the bodies of deeper sea animals, such as the striking green-furred Sea Mouse, a plump, oval-bodied marine worm.

Shingle

All this organic material naturally attracts scavenging animals. Sandhoppers are small crustaceans that live and feed around strandlines. They have great sensitivity to tidal patterns and retreat into burrows at high tide. They, plus the many flies that are attracted to the piles of decaying washed-up material, provide food for birds, such as the Rock Pipit. Other birds that often visit the strandline include Pied Wagtails, Turnstones and various species of crows, and in some areas mammals like Hedgehogs also come and have a look for edible treats among the smelly seaweed. Some extreme high tides may leave enough organic material lying out of the reach of the sea to allow plant communities to begin to become established.

Above The Sea Mouse, a beautiful marine worm, is sometimes discovered as a strandline casualty.

Left Ever the opportunist, a Carrion Crow checks a shingle strandline for edible morsels.

Right With its deep blue flowers and sturdy, spiky shape, Viper's Bugloss is a distinctive shingle plant, and very attractive to insects such as the Essex Skipper butterfly.

Below Yellow Horned Poppies are able to take root in the most unpromising- looking shingly terrain.

PLANTS THAT BIND THE BEACH

Shingle is an even more difficult material for plants to root into than sand, and communities of shingle vegetation comprise a very rare habitat worldwide. Plants that use this habitat need to be resistant to strong winds and sea spray, able to make maximum use of minimal nutrients, and possess a fast-growing and strong root system to hold themselves in place on an inherently loose and easily disturbed substrate. Many shingle beaches have no plant communities at all – those that do are long-established and large beaches, where the action of longshore drift has built up a broad band of beach above the

high water mark and where human disturbance is minimal. Over time, long-established shingle beaches trap smaller sandy and silty particles that can hold fresh water and nutrients in the form of dead seaweed fragments and other organic material. Water and other nutrients are vital to allow plant seeds to germinate and grow. In some areas, the shingle surface lies close to the water table, allowing a plant community more typical of wetlands to develop.

Here are some of the important shingle plants that can be found around Britain.

Oraches *(Atriplex)*
Early colonisers of shingle beach include the oraches, fast-

growing annual plants whose tough seeds may be carried in sea water. These plants grow and die very quickly, and their remains provide a fresh supply of nutrients that other plants are able to exploit.

There are several species of oraches in Britain: all are upright leafy plants with spikes or clusters of small round flowers. They actually look less obviously adapted to the rigours of beach life than some other, less pioneering shingle plants, but as annuals they do not have to survive the harshness of winters on the beach.

Sea Kale *(Crambe maritima)* The cabbage-like Sea Kale has a low profile and thick, tough leaves, making it resistant to exposure to wind and sea water. In summer the low clumps of grey-white leaves are transformed as the abundant white flowers appear. Like the oraches it has large water-bourne seeds, and very long tap roots that push up to 2 metres deep through the shingle to access fresh water.

Yellow Horned Poppy *(Glaucium flavum)* The attractive Yellow Horned Poppy is also a pioneer, though its tiny seeds are dispersed by the wind rather than the sea. It produces large, short-lived bright yellow flowers, which develop into long, tapered seedpods. The leaves are thick with a waxy coating, to minimise water loss.

Sea Bindweed *(Calystegia soldanella)* A relative of the familiar and often unwelcome bindweeds that climb up larger plants in our gardens, Sea Bindweed does not produce spiralling tendrils like its inland cousins, but instead scrambles along and through the shingle. It thrives best in sandy shingle. It produces very pretty trumpet-shaped pink and white flowers, and its scrambling growth form gives it a low profile which helps it to avoid damage from wind.

Viper's Bugloss *(Echium vulgare)* This is one of the most striking and beautiful shingle plants. It grows on more established parts of the beach and also occurs

Shell beaches

A beach composed wholly of washed-up shells is a rare gem in Britain, and indeed worldwide. Such beaches may be made up of the shells of just one mollusc species or several. Like shingle beaches, they tend not to hold as much life as sandy beaches, but are absolutely fascinating spots for the amateur naturalist to explore. Shells, like sand grains and pebbles, settle on shores at spots when the sea's movement is not vigorous enough to hold them in suspension, but only where there are very large concentrations of molluscs can shell beaches form.

Left Winter brings Snow Buntings to both shingle and sandy beaches around the UK, where they forage among the marginal beachside vegetation.

Shingle islands on seaside lagoons are
nesting sites for Black-headed Gulls.

inland. Tall and upright, it produces spikes of bright deep blue flowers with prominently protruding red stamens, and is very attractive to nectar-feeding insects. The slender leaves are very rough and hairy, and it grows very long, deep roots. Viper's Bugloss and Essex Skipper

Right A juvenile Starling looks for food among shingle vegetation.

Below The beautifully streamlined Stoat on a hunt for prey amidst grassy shingle.

Sea Holly (*Eryngium maritimum*)

Not related to the red-berried Holly of gardens and churchyards, this plant is named for its spiky leaves but is actually a member of the carrot family. It prefers sandy shingle at the back of the beach. Deep-rooted, very tough and able to cope with extreme conditions of all kinds, including being buried temporarily by blown sand, this plant produces attractive blue flowers in summer.

ANIMALS OF SHINGLE SHORES

A range of bird species nest on shingle beaches, and there is considerable overlap between shingle and sand beach nesters. The Ringed Plover is probably more at home on shingle than sandy beaches, as its eggs are adapted to resemble stones, and the adults also have a bold,

Bringing back the bees

The last UK record of the Short-haired Bumblebee was in 1988, at Dungeness in Kent. It was declared extinct here in 2000, but does occur elsewhere in Europe, and it was from Sweden that a number of queen bees were taken in 2012, to attempt to re-establish this bee back at Dungeness, a huge shingle peninsula in south Kent. This project is the work of Natural England, the RSPB, the Bumblebee Conservation Trust, and bee and wasp advisory body Hymettus.

Reintroduction is a useful conservation tool, but requires careful planning. If the factors that caused the original extinction are not addressed, then there is every likelihood that the reintroduced stock will also succumb in short order. A key part of the Short-haired Bumblebee project was working with landowners to improve the quality of habitat for the bees, creating new expanses of flower-rich grassland. This part of the project began in 2009 and is ongoing, with more than 850ha of land so far made more bumblebee-friendly.

Deciding where to go for the donor bees was a difficult dilemma. The first choice was, oddly enough, New Zealand, where the Short-tailed Bumblebee is an introduced species. As the bees there descend directly from British ancestors, they seemed a good choice as being genetically similar to the extinct British population, but studies showed that over the 130 years since they were introduced to New Zealand, they had become too inbred to be suitable. Short-haired Bumblebees do occur in much of Europe but are generally declining. Sweden was selected because the species is increasing and spreading there, perhaps indicating a more robust population.

Queen bees were caught in Skane, Sweden, and brought to the UK, and then quarantined for a fortnight to ensure they are healthy and free of parasites, before transportation to the release sites at Dungeness. No worker bees were seen after the 2012 release, so it was not possible to confirm whether any of the queens set up successful nests, but in 2013 a number of workers were seen, indicating that successful nesting had occurred. Another 46 queens were released in spring 2014, and at the time of writing, volunteers are eagerly awaiting the first sightings of worker bees visiting the shingle and grassland flowers.

Shingle

Above Sandwich Terns nest on shingle beaches, but only those that have very little or no human disturbance.

broken pattern that blends in well with the colours of a pebble beach. This is a stocky little short-billed wader, with a distinctive run-pause-run foraging style. Though reliant on camouflage to keep its nest safe, it has another tactic if a mammalian predator, such as a Stoat, has approached too closely. The bird leaves its nest and feigns injury, running and fluttering away from the nest while calling loudly and trailing a wing. With luck, the predator will follow it, and be led a safe distance from the nest before the plover miraculously recovers and flies off.

Terns and some gulls will also nest on shingle. They have well-camouflaged eggs and chicks, but they also use intense co-ordinated mobbing attacks to attempt to drive away predators. However, losses of tern chicks to Foxes, Kestrels and other predators can be very high. While this is natural predation, the terns are at a major disadvantage as there are very few beaches left around British coasts that are sufficiently free from human disturbance to be usable for nesting. Where terns do still nest on mainland beaches, conservation bodies often protect them by erecting

anti-predator fencing, and the provision of artificial shelters where the chicks can hide from aerial dangers.

Shingle plant communities can harbour an interesting range of invertebrate animals. Many of these species are nationally rare, by virtue of the rarity of their habitat. Three bumblebee species are associated with shingle flora – they are the Brown-banded Carder Bee, the Large Garden Bumblebee and the Short-haired Bumblebee.

Other invertebrates associated with coastal vegetated shingle include a number of rarities, such as the

Dark Guest Ant, the bizarre-looking Gilkicker Weevil, and an attractive red true bug, *Rhopalus rufus*. Pools that form between vegetated shingle ridges also hold a range of special invertebrates, including the Medicinal Leech which was believed extinct in Britain before populations were discovered in the Dungeness area.

CONSERVATION OF SHINGLE HABITATS

Vegetated shingle looks a more robust habitat than duneland, but both are vulnerable to damage from erosion. Many dunes under the protection of conservation bodies have boardwalks for visitors to walk on so that they do not trample plants or cause dune ridges to collapse. Some shingle nature reserves have boardwalks too but visitors are less likely to use them, as shingle is more comfortable to walk on than sand. Vehicles can cause serious long-term damage to shingle habitats.

The action of longshore drift can result in natural loss of shingle habitat, and storm surges can push loose shingle up beyond the normal high water mark to smother vegetated areas. In some areas, shingle is extracted for commercial use, or moved from one area to another to counter beach loss from longshore drift – these practices can damage established shingle habitats, as well as prevent future establishment of vegetation.

SHINGLE PITS AND DIGGINGS

Digging out shingle for commercial uses, such as to make aggregate, is inherently

Below A pair of Pikes spawn in a well-established coastal shingle pit.

destructive but can produce new and useful habitats in the form of flooded pits. Many old diggings end up being of considerable wildlife value, and their attractiveness to a wider range of species can be improved through careful management. Many wetland species, both plants and animals, arrive at new pits quickly without any assistance. Insects like dragonflies which have aquatic life-stages travel by air and lay

Left Large-scale shingle-shifting is carried out in some areas to counteract longshore drift and protect against erosion.

their eggs in the water, and amphibians travel on foot. Plant seeds and fish eggs may arrive stuck to water birds' feet, carried on floodwater from nearby rivers, or brought in through streams that join up with the pit. Water birds, even those that like Little Grebes that look barely capable of sustained flight, are remarkably quick to find and investigate new water bodies

Diggings tend to be deep and steep-sided, and as aquatic life begins to colonise them, the pits will attract diving water birds, including Coots, diving ducks,

grebes and (in winter) divers. As pioneer plants become established on the margins, they provide the nutrients that more exacting but longer-lived wetland plants require, and over time the margins of the pit become more sloping through accumulating sediment. This allows a rich marginal vegetation community to develop, and makes the pits hospitable to dabbling ducks and wading birds.

Landscaping and planting can accelerate the process of turning a flooded shingle pit into a lush lake teeming with life. One of the

most valuable extra measures that conservationists can take is to add some shingle islands. These provide nesting places for birds that are much safer than on the lake shore, as they are out of reach to most mammalian predators. Specially designed floating rafts are even more secure than islands as they provide protection from flooding. Species such as Little Ringed Plover and Mediterranean Gull will make use of such islands, alongside more common birds. Artificial banks with built-in nest holes can attract Sand Martins

Below Seaside gravel pits attract lots of wildfowl in winter, including rarer species such as the Goosander.

Left Cormorants have established a small nesting colony on this shingle island in a coastal gravel pit.

and Kingfishers. And because these water bodies are right on the edge of the coast, they often play host to roosting wader flocks at high tide, and to lost and tired seabirds seeking shelter after a storm.

PLACES TO VISIT

Here is a selection of the best shingle beach systems to watch wildlife around the British Isles.

ENGLAND

Dungeness, Kent

A triangular wedge of shingle poking out into the English Channel, the Dungeness peninsula is one of the largest and most important shingle-based ecosystems in Europe. It is designated an NNR, an SPA, an SSSI and an SAC, and it also holds an RSPB reserve, as well

Scrapes and Avocets

On many coastal nature reserves, shallow lagoons provide breeding habitat for an even wider range of bird species. Unlike commercial shingle diggings, these lagoons or scrapes are intended for wildlife from the get-go, and are planned accordingly. The original 'Scrape' was dug at Minsmere RSPB in Suffolk, after an area of land just beyond the beach was deliberately opened up to sea flooding in the 1940s as a wartime defence measure. The flooded area was landscaped by pioneering reserve warden Bert Axell, and the resultant large brackish lagoon, studded with islands, is now home to numerous nesting birds including a substantial population of Avocets. The Avocet, a strikingly elegant pied wader and the RSPB's emblem, was extinct as a breeding bird in Britain until its return to Minsmere and also the nearby Havergate Island in the 1940s. Now it nests on similar scrapes at coastal reserves around much of the southern and eastern English coastline.

Great Black-backed and Herring Gulls
roost on the beach at Dungeness, Kent.

as a bird observatory. The entire area has a huge amount to offer the wildlife-watcher at all times of year, even though at first glance it can seem a bleak and forbidding area – especially when you notice the hulking outline of the nuclear power station on the beach near the tip of the peninsula. The warm-water outflow from the power station attracts fish, which in turn attract masses of gulls and (in summer) terns. These birds swarm over that particular spot of sea (the 'Patch') all day every day. Heading inland, typical shingle vegetation begins to colonise the shingle, and among it live a wide range of invertebrates including many rare species. On the RSPB reserve there are many flooded diggings, both deep and shallow, some reed-fringed, and these play host to many breeding and visiting birds. Ditches between them hold swarms of dragonflies and damselflies in summer, and provide refuges for noisy Marsh Frogs (and hunting grounds for hungry Grass Snakes). The bird observatory benefits from its position near the tip of the headland – newly arrived migrating birds make a bee-line for the vegetated 'moat' that surrounds the observatory building, and numerous rare birds have been trapped and ringed here before being sent on their way.

Chesil Beach, Dorset

This remarkable 29km shingle bar runs in an almost straight line between Portland to Abbotsbury, and encloses a long

Below Chesil Beach in Dorset is the UK's most impressive example of a shingle bar.

tidal lagoon (the Fleet) between itself and the mainland. It is up to 200 metres wide and up to 15 metres high. Its orientation is north-west to south-east, and the shingle that forms in increases in size as you head south-east. Much of Chesil Beach can be accessed freely, but anyone planning to walk its entire length should prepare carefully, as this is a seriously challenging and, at times, risky undertaking. It is part of the Jurassic Coast UNESCO World Heritage Site. The bank itself

Top Black-headed Gulls like to nest on shingle islands and marshland, but can be seen on all coasts outside the breeding season.

Left At Man O' War Bay near Durdle Door in Dorset an extraordinary array of stratified rocks has come to rest vertically after many millennia of earth movements.

plays host to nesting birds including the rare Little Tern, and the Fleet attracts large numbers of feeding waders and wildfowl.

Blakeney Point, Norfolk

An infamous site for birdwatchers, Blakeney Point is a 6.4km spit projecting in a westerly direction, on the north Norfolk coast, made primarily of shingle and sand dunes. Like most such landforms, its exact shape and composition is constantly changing as the sea reshapes the land. Protected as a National Nature Reserve, it is well-known for the many Grey and Common Seals that rest and give birth to their pups on its shores – it is also home to breeding Sandwich Terns, Mediterranean Gulls and many other species. Boat trips run out to the point to see the wildlife, and it can be reached on foot if you can face the long trek. However access is very limited, you may not walk to the end in summer (to protect nesting birds) and late autumn-early winter (to prevent disturbance to seals). Full access in spring and autumn is of benefit to keen birdwatchers, who visit in migration season in the hope of finding rare migrant birds taking refuge here.

Shellness, Kent

The beach at the eastern tip of the Isle of Sheppey is composed not of shingle but of shells, mainly cockles. This in itself makes the beach a very interesting place to visit, but it is also part of the Swale nature reserve and is particularly good to visit in winter, when the shell beach hosts a large wader roost. Arrive ahead of high tide and you could see masses of Dunlins, Grey Plovers, Sanderlings, Knots, Bar-tailed Godwits, Oystercatchers and other shorebirds, as well as flocks of Brent Geese. The area understandably also attracts many birds of prey, with Short-eared Owls patrolling the grazing marsh behind the beach, and Peregrines and Merlins 'buzzing' the roosting shorebirds. Snow Buntings and Shore Larks may forage on the strandline.

Far left The shell beach at Shellness, Kent, attracts a large wader roost in winter. Here, Bar-tailed Godwits join a group of Oystercatchers.

Left Rocky breakwaters on shingle beaches offer roosting and feeding sites for Purple Sandpipers.

WALES

Cemlyn, Anglesey

This is an important nature reserve, managed by the Wales Wildlife Trust and part of the Anglesey AONB. A shingle ridge separates a large lagoon from the sea, and here you will find one of the UK's most important colonies of Sandwich Terns, as well as Common and Arctic Terns and Ringed Plovers, while you may see a Chough overhead if you are lucky. The shingle holds an interesting vegetation community.

SCOTLAND

Spey Bay, Highland

This is Scotland's largest shingle beach and lies at the mouth of the Spey, a large and fast-flowing river which casts its wide influence across the landscape for many kilometres inland, cutting out a beautiful and ecologically rich valley though the towering Cairngorms. Spey Bay is managed by the Scotland Wildlife Trust, and the higher parts of its shingle beach hosts a colourful array of plants in summer, including several species of orchids, and Kidney Vetch, an attractive yellow-flowered plant which attracts the delicate Small Blue butterfly. Ospreys regularly fish in the bay in summer, and you may also see Otters coming ashore with their catches of fish or crabs. Offshore, the famous Bottlenose Dolphins of the Moray Firth are regularly seen.

IRELAND

Dunbeacon Shingle, Co Cork

This small but diverse site is designated an SAC, and is protected as a nature reserve. It has a good community of shingle vegetation with associated invertebrates, and there is also saltmarsh and dry heath here to explore. Little Egrets, still rare in Ireland, regularly visit to feed, and Otters also occur.

Carlingford Shore, Co Louth

This is a beautiful and dramatic shoreline, flanked by mountains, and with a broad shingle ridge hosting a wide range of perennial vegetation on its higher areas as well as annual plants on the strandline. A scarce plant found here is the pretty Oysterplant, also known as Sea Bluebell. The area is important for its birdlife, including large numbers of Brent Geese (of the pale-bellied form) in winter, while Grey Seals haul out on banks offshore. A number of Black Guillemots sometimes nest on artificial structures such as breakwaters.

Far left A view across Spey Bay, Highland.

Above Oystercatchers' eggs are well camouflaged on a shingle beach.

Left Look out for the blue flowers of Oysterplant at Carlingford Shore, Co. Louth.

Estuary

Where river meets sea, some very distinct habitat types develop. Rivers carry masses of sediment towards the sea, and this sediment contains plenty of organic material that serves as food for marine plants and small animals – these in turn attract larger animals. The mudflats that form around sheltered estuaries are magnetically attractive to wildfowl and shorebirds, which can congregate in mind-boggling numbers, and the birds of prey that come to hunt them. The mud teems with small burrowing animals, and the tidal reaches of the river, where fresh and salt water mingle, have their own specialised wildlife communities. The influence of the sea on the river and its wildlife can reach more than 100km inland. Many estuaries around Britain have lost some of their wildlife interest as a result of development, but nature reserves protect some key sites, and some estuarine areas are internationally important for their wildlife. Walking around wild estuaries can be hazardous because of the soft muddy ground, but they are magnificent landscapes, with their big skies and expansive mudflats, with vast flocks of waders and wildfowl circling above.

RIVER VERSUS SEA

Rivers and streams begin their lives well inland, often on high ground, and their source point may derive from marshland, a lake, melting glacial ice or natural springs of underground water. As they flow seawards, small streams converge with larger ones, and the growing river has an increasingly noticeable impact on surrounding land, carving out channels through hard rock, and building sediment-rich floodplains as it nears the sea.

As the tide goes in, salt water is pushed into river mouths, and comes into contact with the fresh water flowing down the river. Because fresh water is less dense than water carrying dissolved salt, in very sheltered conditions there are distinct layers of fresh and salt water in estuaries, but water movement usually mixes the two to produce brackish water, which is salty but less so than sea water. How salty the water in an estuary is varies through the day as the tide changes, but also through the

year. Higher rainfall in winter means a higher output of fresh water, but in a dry summer estuarine water becomes much saltier as river outflow is reduced. The river and sea generate opposing currents, meaning estuary water can be turbulent and dangerous. In a few estuaries, such as the Severn, the geomorphology encourages the development of 'tidal bores' – large, powerful rolling waves that travel upriver, posing considerable danger for shipping but providing the

Below

Estuaries have long been of great importance for industry, and more recently also for leisure pursuits – including wildlife-watching.

opportunity for the dramatic sport of river surfing. Tidal bores also help to aerate the water, which helps encourage wildlife.

Estuaries come in several forms. 'Coastal plain' estuaries form where rising sea levels have flooded or 'drowned' an unglaciated, lowland river valley. From an aerial view they usually show a tree-like form. The estuary of the River Fal in Cornwall is a good example of this estuary type, and most other estuaries on the south coast of England are the same kind. 'Fjord' estuaries form on northern, rocky coasts and have steep banks without associated mudflats. Many firths and sea lochs in Scotland are fjord

estuaries – their coastlines are not very different to sea-facing rocky shores or cliffs, although their water is less saline. A third kind of estuary is 'bar-built', where barrier beaches or spits of shingle and sand enclose much of the estuary, forming a lagoon which shrinks or completely empties at low tide, leaving exposed muddy shores. The Alde/Ore/Butley estuary complex in Suffolk is an example of this type.

MUD-RUNNERS

Around the coast of the British Isles, there are a number of particularly large and ecologically rich estuaries which are effectively service stations

for the thousands of shorebirds that migrate from the Arctic to temperate areas (and in some cases as far the southern hemisphere) and back every year. Some wader species do breed in Britain and can be seen at estuaries all year round, but their numbers are dwarfed by the migrants and those that stay with us over winter.

Autumn migration along our shores is more pronounced, more prolonged and involves far more birds than does the return spring migration. This is because the flocks are in no great hurry to reach their wintering grounds, and are near the start of their journey so need to take on plenty of fuel. Numbers are at their

parts of the estuary soon get covered by water, obliging the birds to move to other areas. If the entire estuary fills up, which may only happen on the biggest spring tides, the birds find a safe place above the high water mark, and sleep for the few hours that they cannot feed. Several nature reserves near estuaries have created artificial lagoons with islands, which waders use as safe high-tide roosting places.

To a hungry bird of prey, the great concentrations of waders represent an abundant food supply, and it would seem that even the most inexperienced raptor couldn't fail to catch one bird from the huge numbers

Above
Although it is a small wader, the Curlew Sandpiper's relatively long legs and bill make it well adapted to probe soft estuarine mud.

highest because the flocks hold not just the adult birds that have finished breeding, but a whole new generation of youngsters. In spring, numbers have been reduced, the journey is almost complete, and the birds are also eager to reach the breeding grounds and claim a territory, so tend not to dawdle on the way. Some species that stop off at our shores in good numbers in autumn are hardly seen at all in spring.

Waders choose their activities by the tides, rather than the day-night cycle. They are very happy to feed through the darkest night hours if feeding is possible. At low tide they spread out across the expanse of exposed muddy shore. The incoming tide pushes them in and bunches them up. Some

Washed out

One of Britain's most important estuary complexes is the Wash in east England, and as well as attracting hundreds of thousands of feeding waders, in winter it also serves as vital habitat for nearly 100,000 Pink-footed Geese. The geese disperse across Norfolk and neighbouring counties in the daytime, but the Wash is effectively their holiday hotel, offering not feeding grounds but a safe place for them to roost through the long winter nights. Whatever the tide is doing they can take shelter in this huge bay of mud and shallow water, safe in the knowledge that no Fox or other land predator is likely to try to reach them. Well before first light, the flocks are waking, their ringing, bugling calls betraying their presence across the darkness of the estuary, and as the sunrise begins to touch the edge of the sky they start to lift off, flying inland in long strings and straggly V-formations to begin their day of foraging in the rich farmland fields of the East Anglian fens.

Estuary

available. The waders have a defence mechanism though. When they see a raptor approaching, the whole flock takes to the air, and performs spectacular synchronous manoeuvres, so they become a twisting ball or ribbon of fast-flickering movement, and tracking any one individual becomes incredibly difficult. The raptor's best chance then is zeroing in on any bird which doesn't quite keep up with the flock's moves. Peregrine Falcon is the raptor that you are most likely to see trying its luck on a wader flock, but the much smaller Merlin will also attack small waders like Dunlins.

For resting and feeding waders, energy is at a premium, especially as they are likely to be forced into the air by birds of prey from time to time. It is therefore very important that you take care not to disturb them – don't approach too closely, and keep dogs under close control when walking near flocks of waders. There are several superb nature reserves where

Top It is important to avoid disturbing waders when they are roosting or feeding, especially in winter.

Left A Sanderling interrupts its shoreline feeding and moves up to dry ground to briefly sleep.

Overleaf A flock of Knots takes flight. By moving as one, the birds may confuse and disorientate a potential predator.

to probe or pick at the ground. Dunlins are very widespread outside the breeding season and may be encountered on any flat muddy shoreline and river mouth. Only small numbers breed in Britain (primarily on inland moors) – many that visit Britain have travelled from Greenland, Iceland, Russia and even Canada.

Knot *(Calidris canutus)*

The most impressive formation-flying wader flocks you can see around Britain are flocks of Knots, and some of the congregations hold tens of thousands of birds, though

Above The commonest small estuary wader is the Dunlin. When it is in summer plumage, its black belly-patch is diagnostic.

Right Redshanks are common on estuaries all year round, as well as on other low-lying coastal habitat.

waders can be observed at close quarters from hides without risk of disturbance, while the birds are at their high-tide roosts.

ESTUARINE WADERS

Here are some of the waders you are likely to find feeding in the intertidal zone around our estuaries.

Dunlin *(Calidris alpina)* This is the 'default small wader', squat and shortish-legged with a downcurved bill and, in winter, rather plain light brown plumage on its upperside and a white underside. In the breeding season, it becomes more colourful, with reddish tones on its upperparts, and a black belly-patch. Its restless feeding action is sometimes likened to a sewing machine, walking along while constantly dipping its head

smaller flocks are also seen. The Knot is a fairly small but stout and solid wader, with rather featureless pale grey plumage in winter, which turns to brown and brick-red in summer. When searching for food it marches along with head bowed, ready to snap at prey with its relatively short bill. Our Knots come mainly from Arctic Canada, and make their way to Britain via Iceland. Some of the birds continue on from here to other European estuaries, but more than 300,000 birds stick around throughout winter.

Redshank (Tringa totanus)

With its ringing call, this wader is nicknamed 'the sentinel of the marshes', and it can be seen around estuaries all year round as well as on coastal marshland, where it nests. It is medium-sized and slim, with an elegant way of moving and striking bright red legs, plus broad white trailing edges to its wings which show in flight. Redshanks will flock when not breeding, but you are just as likely to see them singly, moving along shore edges or wading in shallow water. They probe the mud for worms but will also chase insects and even tiny fish.

Curlew (Numenius arquata)

The biggest wader you'll see on the estuary, this sturdy all-brown bird can give the impression of a very leggy juvenile gull, especially in flight, until you catch a glimpse of its tremendously long, downcurved bill. The bill size varies with age and by sex, with mature females boasting the most impressive mud-probing equipment. This bird is often seen singly, dwarfing the other waders around, and its mournful 'coor-lee' call is one of the most beautiful sounds of the estuary. In spring and summer, you may also hear its extraordinary rippling song, although most of Britain's breeding Curlews nest inland, on heaths, moorlands and grassland. In spring particularly, beware confusing Curlews with migrant Whimbrels (*Numenius phaeopus*), which are smaller with bills that look 'kinked' rather than smoothly downcurved, and prominent striped head markings.

Bar-tailed Godwit (Limosa lapponica)

In its streaky brown winter plumage, this large wader looks rather like a straight-billed, small Curlew. However, in spring

Above With their overly long, curved bills, Curlews are consummate mud-probers.

Above The
rescue team work
to save the
'Thames Whale'.

and autumn, at least some
individuals will show signs of the
attractive orange-red breeding
plumage. These godwits do not
breed in Britain, but nest on
remote tundra near the Arctic
circle. The closely related
Black-tailed Godwit (*Limosa
limosa*) is a similarly large and
long-billed bird but has clearly
longer legs as well as various
subtle plumage differences. It is
also more likely to be found on
freshwater coastal marshes than
on the actual shoreline.

Grey Plover *(Pluvialis squatarola)*

With its distinctive large-headed,
short-billed shape, and habit of
standing stock-still with head
raised before making a short,
darting run, this plover cuts a
striking figure among the other
shoreline waders. Seen well, it is
very beautiful with spangled
silvery plumage, and in summer
it has a black face and underside.
At all times of year it shows neat
black 'armpit' patches in flight.
Grey Plovers may be found on
sandy and stony shores as well
as on muddy estuaries, and
unlike the longer-billed waders
they find prey by sight rather
than by touch. Nesting in the
Arctic, they begin to arrive as
early as July, and while many
stay through the winter, some

continue southwards to winter on
the African coast.

Other waders that you might see
around estuaries include
Sanderlings, Oystercatchers and
Turnstones, but these are more
closely associated with other
coastal habitats, and all are
described in more detail
elsewhere in this book.

SURPRISES IN THE RIVER

In January 2006, Londoners were
astounded to see a whale
swimming in the Thames. The
story of the female Northern
Bottlenose Whale made
international headlines, and

many people witnessed the (sadly unsuccessful) attempt by the British Divers Marine Life Rescue to rescue the clearly unwell animal and return it to the sea. The whale died two days after it was first seen in the river, and its skeleton is now in the possession of the Natural History Museum.

This was an exceptional event, but it is not unusual for smaller sea mammals and pelagic seabirds to enter river mouths from time to time, and most will not come to any harm as a result. At RSPB Rainham Marshes on the north shore of the Thames, more than 30km upriver from the open sea, it is not unusual to see both Common and Grey Seals hauled out on the foreshore, and Harbour Porpoises and Bottlenose Dolphins have both been seen in the river. Dolphins and porpoises are most likely to swim upriver at high tide, and will leave again as the tide goes out. They are attracted by congregations of fish in the estuarine waters, and alongside them may be good numbers of fish-eating water birds, such as divers, grebes and mergansers. Even the Kingfisher will head downstream from its preferred inland habitats to find fishing grounds around estuaries in winter, especially during a freeze.

Seabirds which are normally pelagic (not found inland at all) sometimes travel up river mouths in search of shelter from severe weather. Such events are most likely in autumn, when more seabirds are on the move anyway as they disperse away from their breeding grounds. The species most likely to be affected are smaller seabirds. The 'holy trinity' of scarce wanderers that are prone to flying upriver in autumn gales are the Grey Phalarope, Leach's Storm-petrel, and Sabine's Gull, none of which are easy to see for British birders under normal circumstances, as they normally migrate past us some distance offshore.

The most remarkable record of a seabird heading inland took place in Kent in autumn 2009. Strictly speaking, the Swale is not a river but a 20km channel, as it divides the Isle of Sheppey from the mainland, but at its western end it feeds into the River Medway, and it is barely more than 70 metres across along much of its length. Birdwatchers in the shoreside hide at Oare Marshes Nature

Reserve on 16 September 2009 must have wondered if their flasks of coffee had been spiked when they saw a Tufted Puffin, a species native to the north Pacific, come flying up the channel. The bird, the first of its kind ever seen in Britain, rested on the water for a while before flying on, but was not seen again, and the many birders who travelled to Kent in the hope of refinding it had to leave disappointed.

Below The Tufted Puffin has to be one of the most improbable bird species to have found itself on the British list.

Left Grey Phalaropes are really open-sea birds when not breeding, but severe weather at sea pushes them into sheltered estuaries.

FEELING THE PRESSURE

People have been establishing substantial settlements around estuaries for thousands of years. Easy access to fresh water for drinking and the sea for trade and travel makes them convenient places to establish towns and cities. Another advantage is that rivers on low ground near the sea create expanses of flat fertile land, good for farming, while there is an abundance of 'wild' food in the form of fish and birdlife. Some of the world's oldest known settlements were around estuaries, as are many large modern cities today.

Development of estuaries is damaging to wildlife and ecosytems in a number of ways. Often, dredging of mud and silt from the river mouth and sea bed takes place, making them deeper and more easily navigable by boat. The reclaimed sediment is used to build up the edges of the estuary, creating new, higher land which can then be built upon. This obviously removes the mudflats that hold such richly diverse invertebrate life, and make the estuary much less attractive to wading birds. It also makes the land adjoining the estuary more susceptible to flooding during storm surges, and exposes the newly reclaimed land to erosion by wave action.

Estuaries can also suffer from heavy pollution, from both the sea and the river, and because of the sediment-depositing nature of typical estuaries, pollutants can linger and accumulate in the intertidal area and have a profound effect on the estuarine wildlife, especially molluscs such as cockles and mussels, which feed by filtering out organic material from the water. As favoured areas for fishing, estuaries can be overfished to the point where they have little left to offer fish-eating birds and mammals.

Below
A dredger in the Bristol Channel.

Left Most
south-coast
estuaries provide
homes for people
rather than wildlife.
This is Dartmouth
in Devon.

species of organisms can do it. However, they make up for their lack of variety by proliferating in huge numbers. Mudshrimps and the tiny snail *Hydrobia ulvae* can be present in their thousands in every handful of mud. Living within the mud are various species of cockles, and the Ragworm makes its burrows 20cm deep. This worm's 10cm body is covered in long bristles, giving it the look of a frayed piece of cloth, and interestingly it

Virtually all of the sizeable estuaries around the British Isles now have some degree of development, many are very extensive developed. The amount of wildlife habitat that has been lost, especially over the last century, is huge. The pressure is still high today, with companies constantly seeking permission for new developments to estuarine areas. Perhaps the most high-profile proposal in the 21st century so far has been the idea of building a new hub airport in the Thames estuary – a move which has been strongly resisted by the RSPB and other bodies involved with conservation. Many recent building developments on estuaries have only gained approval on the condition that new habitat is created nearby to compensate for that which is being lost.

LIFE IN THE MUD

Living permanently in or on thick, oxygen-poor mud is quite a challenge and not very many

Rebuilding the past

Protecting remnants of prime estuary habitat from further development is a high priority of British conservation bodies, and in some areas the efforts are going beyond mere preservation and seeking to restore and recreate estuarine habitats. One example of this process is the Wallasea Wild Coast project, in Essex, where the RSPB and other partners are working to restore a huge area of rich intertidal habitat. Wallasea Island's exposure to the sea was drastically reduced when sea walls were built, and its wet pastures were drained to make the land suitable for arable use in the 1930s. By allowing the sea to breach defences, the farmland will return to marshland, and the intertidal parts of the site will be landscaped for maximum habitat diversity using spoil from the tunnelling that is underway to develop the Crossrail underground train links. A similarly ambitious RSPB 'Futurescapes' project focuses on the Inner Forth in eastern Scotland. As well as creating superb wildlife habitat, these projects aim to make the areas in question highly accessible to visitors, to ensure that the new opportunities for wildlife-watching can help improve the local economy and quality of life.

Below The
colourful Shelduck
is a classic
estuarine bird.

Right Brent Geese are winter visitors to Britain and are almost entirely dependent on eelgrasses.

Below The tiny Hydrobia snails that burrow into estuary mud are important foodstuffs for a range of larger animals.

changes colour from brown to green before the start of its breeding season. It feeds on all kinds of organic matter, which it extracts from the water by spinning a 'net' from mucous at the top of its burrow, then drawing water into its burrow through the net by squirming vigorously. It then eats the net, plus any edible particles caught in it, before making a new net. Ragworms are used as bait by fishers, and relished by wading birds. The presence of ragworms can slow down plant colonisation of estuarine mudflats, as the worms eat the plants.

Right Eelgrass grows in the shallows of a tidal pool.

The first plant to set up home in wet muddy estuaries are the eelgrasses, often known by their genus name *Zostera*. They are slim, grass-like plants, but are not actually true grasses. Common Eelgrass can live and grown on mud that is under sea water most of the time, and establishes underwater 'meadows' in calm estuarine lagoons, spreading via horizontally creeping rhizomes. Its fronds provide shelter for the young fry of various marine fishes. Many animals feed on its leaves, most notably the Brent Goose, our most marine species of goose.

Among the first land plants to colonise estuary margins and begin to establish saltmarsh are the cordgrasses, genus *Spartina*. These plants tolerate saline conditions, possessing the ability to excrete surplus salt, and their masses of fine roots provide strong anchorage in soft ground. Our native cordgrass, *Spartina maritima*, has been pushed out of some of its habitats by a hybrid form called *S. anglica*, the result of crosses between *S. maritima* and the introduced North American *S. alterniflora*. The hybrid form is a vigorous and effective colonist, and in some areas it has spread very widely

Estuary

across mudflats and deprived wading birds of feeding habitat.

Pioneering vegetation on the estuary edge traps sediment, and gradually the land level rises, bringing it above the normal reach of the sea. This opens the door for many new species of plants to colonise, including grasses like Sea Couch, and flowering plants including Sea Aster. This habitat teems with invertebrates, including rarities like the attractive, iridescent Saltmash Shortspur Beetle. Saltmarsh also provides a natural defence against flooding – but man-made sea defences often interfere with the natural development of saltmarsh, by preventing sediment deposition and allowing increased erosion.

PLACES TO VISIT

Here is a selection of the best estuarine areas to watch wildlife around the British Isles.

ENGLAND

Hayle Estuary, Cornwall

The north coast of Cornwall is mainly rocky, punctuated with sandy bays, so this rather small but very rich estuary is a real magnet for shorebirds in the area. Its position at the south-western tip of England also means it often plays host to lost migrant waders, ducks and gulls from North America, and it also regularly attracts unusual large wading birds, such as Spoonbills. Taking the railway between St Erth and St Ives gives wonderful views across the estuary, and the RSPB has a hide at the site overlooking Ryan's field, where a pool with islands is used as a high-tide roost by waders. Nearby is Carnsew Pool, a deeper lake not connected to the River Hayle, where divers and

Below
Farlington Marshes in Hampshire holds an important expanse of saltmarsh habitat.

and Brent Geese in autumn and winter. An important colony of Little Terns nests here.

Snettisham, Norfolk

This RSPB reserve on the north-west Norfolk coast offers some astounding estuarine wildlife-watching if you time your visit just right. It adjoins the Wash, and from the paths around the reserve you can look out over the endless mudflats, and probably find wading birds dotted around, some near and some far. As the tide comes in, the birds are pushed inshore, and on the highest tides they leave the mud altogether and take refuge on islands and banks on lagoons on the other side of the path, where they can be watched from hides. The reserve is also a perfect spot to watch Pink-footed Geese in their thousands, as they arrive to roost at dusk, or set off again at dawn. The reserve at Snettisham suffered some damage after the storm surges of winter 2013– 2014, and at the time of writing some of the trails are still closed.

Above The Hayle estuary, in west Cornwall.

Right Little Terns may be seen fishing in the mouth of Pagham Harbour, West Sussex.

grebes hunt for fish along with the occasional displaced seabird.

Pagham Harbour, West Sussex

Once a river valley, Pagham Harbour is a natural harbour and the smallest of the various harbours on the English coast along the Solent. It is one of the less developed estuaries on the south coast of England, and one of the easiest for wildlife-watchers to explore. It is an SSSI, an SPA and a Ramsar site and is managed as a nature reserve by the RSPB. Expanses of mud are revealed at low tide, which attracts masses of waders

Slimbridge WWT, Gloucestershire

The Severn estuary is a key habitat for wading birds and wildfowl, and there are important nature reserves covering parts of the mudflats on both sides of the river. Slimbridge, run by the Wildfowl and Wetlands Trust, is probably the best known. Part of the site is used to house a collection of exotic captive wildfowl, and also has aviaries where threatened species are being captive-bred prior to reintroduction projects. Common Cranes first bred here are now nesting wild in the local area. Slimbridge also has nature trails leading alongside lakes and ditches and finally to the estuary itself, and from these you can see spectacular numbers of wading birds and wildfowl in autumn and winter.

Parkgate, Cheshire

The Dee estuary, marking the border between north Wales and England, is a superb birdwatching area, with extensive areas of mudflat and saltmarsh, and there are a number of nature reserves on both the English and the Welsh side. Parkgate is famous for offering an extraordinary spectacle at the highest tides, when the saltmarsh is

Below Pagham Harbour on a winter afternoon.

Below When the marsh is inundated during big tides at Parkgate, Cheshire, Short-eared Owls swoop on voles as they flee the oncoming sea-water.

completely inundated and flocks of birds that are pushed off the mudflats and marshland fly very close to observers. A number of small mammals are also forced to rush landward to escape the rising tide, and in winter attendant birds of prey such as Hen Harriers and Short-eared Owls will come to the estuary to hunt them.

Morecambe Bay, Lancashire/ Cumbria

Five large rivers drain into this huge estuary complex, the largest area of tidal mudflats in the UK. Much of the area has been developed and altered, and the bay has multiple uses including a major cockle-picking industry, but it remains hugely important for wildlife. It is best known for its birdlife, and holds many thousands of Knots, Oystercatchers, Dunlins, Lapwings, Wigeons and Shelducks, with smaller numbers of other species. Viewing the wildlife of the bay can be difficult as it is such a vast area, but the RSPB's Leighton Moss reserve on the Lancashire side of the bay includes hides looking over part of the bay. On the other side, Cumbria Wildlife

Estuary

Trust manages Humphrey Head reserve, a limestone outcrop into the bay which offers wonderful views and is also home to its own interesting range of plantlife.

SCOTLAND

Mersehead, Dumfries and Galloway

The Solway Firth divides Scotland and England on the west side of Britain, and is important for its visiting flocks of Barnacle Geese. This beautiful small goose is rare in Britain generally but spectacular numbers congregate on the Solway Firth in winter, and can

Above **Morecambe Bay in Lancashire.**

Left **Huge numbers of Shelducks spend their winters at Morecambe Bay.**

be seen from RSPB Mersehead, as well as the Wildfowl and Wetlands Trust's reserve at Caerlaverock. Waders feed on the estuary shore at low tide in winter, while when the tide is high you may see seaduck and other diving waterfowl swimming by at close range.

Nigg and Udale Bay, Highland

These two bays are situated on the north and south sides respectively of the Cromarty Firth, and both are managed as wildlife reserves by the RSPB. The Cromarty Firth is a relatively small offshoot of the Moray Firth, and is sheltered by two tall headlands that guard its entrance. The firth as a whole is fairly unspoilt and is an SPA. At Nigg Bay, allowing the sea to breach coastal defences has helped to convert reclaimed farmland back to intertidal habitats which attract waders and wildfowl. Eelgrass grows prolifically here and attracts large numbers of Wigeons and Whooper Swans, while waders feed on the open exposed mud. At high tide, there is a chance of seeing seals and cetaceans in the firth as well as seaducks and other diving seabirds.

Skinflats, Falkirk

This RSPB reserve is part of the Inner Forth 'Futurescapes' development project (see above), and consists of a large area of intertidal mudflats and a smaller area of saltmarsh. It attracts impressive flocks of Pink-footed

Below A cold day at Mersehead, Dumfries and Galloway.

Geese, plus other wildfowl and waders. This site can at present be viewed from public footpaths, but over years to come there will be more facilities added and the site will be expanded.

Loch Sunart, Argyll

A fjord-type estuary into which many streams and rivers empty, the lovely 31km-long Loch Sunart marks the southern shore of the Ardnamurchan peninsula, one of the wildest parts of the UK and home to a huge range of wildlife. The loch, best explored in summer and by boat, is home to Otters and

Harbour Porpoises, and both White-tailed and Golden Eagles regularly fly overhead. Look into the water below and you should see masses of Moon Jellyfish, and perhaps also the impressive red-tentacled Lion's Mane Jellyfish. The rocky shores of the loch have nesting Shags in some places.

WALES

Dyfi Estuary, Ceredigion

This SPA site is part of the more extensive Dyfi NNR, which includes the Ynyslas dune system mentioned in chapter 1,

and the inland peat mire of Cors Fochno. The estuary around the mouth of the river Dyfi is partly managed by the RSPB and is of particular importance for the Greenland White-fronted Geese that visit in winter. A pair of Ospreys have nested upstream by the Dyfi since 2011, one of the first pairs to breed in Wales for more than 100 years. The incumbent pair, plus increasing numbers of interlopers interested in taking over their nest, can be seen fishing in the estuary through spring and summer, taking sea fish such as Flounder, Sea Bass and Mullet.

Above Loch Sunart is remote, beautiful, and a wonderful area for wildlife-watching.

Right The Dyfi estuary in Ceredigion is a great place to watch Ospreys fishing.

Below Estuaries in Ireland often attract vagrant waders from North America, such as the Pectoral Sandpiper.

IRELAND

Lough Foyle, Co Donegal/Co Londonderry

This sea lough is an SPA and a Ramsar site, and is very important for the wildfowl and shorebirds that use it in autumn and winter. It covers a vast area but some of the best parts can be viewed from paths along the south-eastern shore, where the RSPB manages an area as a nature reserve. There are extensive 'meadows' of eelgrass here which attract wild swans and geese, as well as Wigeons and other dabbling ducks.

Waders feed on the mudflats, and a number of birds of prey such as Peregrines, Merlins and Short-eared Owls haunt the whole area.

Rogerstown Estuary, Co Dublin

This estuary on Ireland's east coast is a Ramsar site, designated because of its importance for wildfowl and waders as a refuelling stop on their north–south migrations. Part of the estuary is managed by Birdwatch Ireland as a nature reserve, and there are hides on both the northern and southern shores of the inner part of the estuary, affording excellent views of the birds. The site regularly attracts several North American species such as Pectoral Sandpipers, American Wigeons and Green-winged Teals.

Moy Estuary, Co Sligo/Co Mayo

A sheltered estuary in eastern Ireland, this site has extensive mudflats, which have eelgrass mats in some areas, and also areas of saltmarsh. It is a Ramsar site and an SPA, important for wintering and passage birdlife including high numbers of Dunlins, Bar-tailed Godwits, Golden Plovers and Lapwings. It is possible to visit the estuary by boat, and gain close views of the Grey Seals that are present in the estuary all year round.

Above A boat trip around the Moy estuary in eastern Ireland offers the chance to enjoy close views of Grey Seals.

Wetlands

Lagoons, lakes, ditches and wet meadows along low-lying coasts mark the next stage in the transition from sea to land. These lush landscapes may hold saline, brackish or fresh water, and are often associated with the lower, tidal reaches of rivers and with estuaries. This kind of marshy habitat is characterised by a lack of trees and sizeable shrubs, and a great abundance of herbaceous plants. While marshland also exists inland, coastal marshes and wetlands are generally more extensive and more species-rich, offering some of the best wildlife-watching you'll find anywhere. Most coastal habitats have a 'best season to visit' – for example, cliffs thronged with birds and topped with colourful flowers can be bleak and quiet in winter, while mudflats hold masses of birdlife in winter but far less in summer. However, coastal marshes are full of interest at all times of year.

94

SUCCESSFUL SUCCESSION

As a saltmarsh builds up sediment (something that the *Spartina* cordgrasses assist with very efficiently) and lifts itself beyond the reach of the sea, it becomes inundated less often by salt water and can be colonised by plants that need drier conditions and lower salinity. The same goes for the margins of the tidal stretches of rivers and their associated creeks. One of the key fringing plants in wetlands, both brackish and fresh, is the Common Reed, a tall grass with large, loose flowerheads. This plant grows densely in muddy margins, forming reedbeds, which are vital habitat for a wide range of animals both small and large. Other plants that take advantage of similar conditions include sedges, rushes and their relatives. The impressive Common Reedmace (sometimes known as Bulrush) is one of the most distinctive with its brown, sausage-shaped flowerheads. Another very striking wetland plant that grows in profusion at the edges of water is the Yellow Flag Iris, which puts on a stunning show of colour in early summer.

Over time, reedbeds and wetland fringes naturally dry out, as leaf litter from the plants builds up, and sediment accumulates. The drier ground is suitable for a different range of plants, which gradually take over, shrinking the area of open water, and in due course what used to be a wetland becomes a woodland. This is a natural process, but by interfering in the early stages of wetland development (by controlling sea and river erosion and deposition processes) we limit the generation of new marshes to replace those that naturally dry out. Therefore, intensive management takes place on the many marshy nature reserves along our coasts, to prevent

Below Reedmace flower heads turn from smooth sausages to fluffballs in autumn, as their hairy seeds develop.

vegetation succession and keep this rare habitat as it is.

Management involves controlling water levels via sluices, and clearing leaf litter away from the bases of the reedbeds. It may also include digging new ditches and areas of open water where marshland vegetation can become established. Many animals of marshland need a mosaic of habitats – for example, Bitterns need older, drier reedbeds in which to nest, but require open, deeper water in which to hunt fish. Management often means deploying heavy machinery to dig and cut, but traditional reed-cutting also takes place (and produces thatching material), and livestock are used to graze marshy grassland. They can control scrub growth and their hooves break up the ground layer of vegetation, allowing a wider range of seeds to germinate. This helps to help produce a variety of habitat types.

REEDBED BIRDS

Through the last few decades, conservation bodies in Britain have invested a great deal of time, effort and money in projects to protect and improve existing areas of extensive reedbeds, and to create new areas of reedbed. As a result, rare birds that depend on this particular habitat have increased in population and greatly expanded their breeding distribution. Other commoner reedbed birds have also benefited.

Bittern *(Botaurus stellaris)*

Extinct in Britain at the start of the 20th century, this stocky, streaky brown heron made a comeback a few decades later, but it has been hanging by a thread through most of the last century. By the mid-1990s, the number of breeding pairs barely reached double figures. Since

Above

Above
Reedbeds are important wildlife habitat and home to many rare and charismatic species.

Konik ponies

Choosing the right livestock to help keep the marshland marshy requires a bit of thought. There are several breeds of ponies native to the British Isles, but they are adapted to live in dry and often upland terrain. To find an equine that is suited to wetlands, it was necessary to look further afield.

Konik ponies originated in Poland. They have a distinctive look, with a light buff-grey body coat and darker manes, tails, legs and muzzles (a colour combination known as 'blue dun' in horse parlace). In their home country they are scarce but increasing, and have the run of several national parks. The Wildwoods Trust, a Kent-based organisation concerned with conservation of European mammals, spearheaded plans to bring some Koniks to Britain and use them to help restore and maintain wetland habitat, and today several nature reserves use the horses in this way. The Koniks seem more than happy with this arrangement, and can be seen at reserves like RSPB Loch of Strathbeg in Aberdeenshire and Blacktoft Sands in East Yorkshire.

Another animal sometimes used to provide habitat management through grazing at wetland sites is the Water Buffalo, a domesticated animal native to the Indian subcontinent. It relishes the opportunity to laze around in a marshy pool and so settles well in the wettest of wetlands, although some British cattle breeds can do as good a job.

Below Konik ponies (right) and Water Buffalos (left) are both used for grazing on wetland nature reserves.

that low point, though, it has done much better and there are now getting on for 100 pairs, some inland but many on coastal wetlands. Bitterns are shy and furtive birds, but the males give themselves away with their breathy 'booming' territorial call, and from hides on nature reserves like RSPB Minsmere you stand a fair chance of seeing one slinking out of the reeds to fish at the water's edge. In winter, several hundred extra Bitterns visit Britain from the continent, sometimes more if there is a big freeze across mainland Europe. These birds will make use of quite small reedbeds, as they do not need a territory large enough to support a breeding attempt.

Marsh Harrier *(Circus aeruginosus)*

Unlike the Bittern, the Marsh Harrier did not go extinct in Britain but came as close as it could have, with just one active nest in the whole of the British Isles in the early 1970s. Its recovery since then has been spectacular, and today there are about 400 pairs. It has also spread from its east-coast stronghold to colonise coastal marshland in parts of Wales and Scotland. Although a nationally rare bird still, it is the easiest bird of prey to see at many coastal marshes, cutting a distinctive shape as it glides low over the reeds on bowed wings, using the breeze to give it enough lift to maintain a slow flight as it

searches for small mammals, birds and amphibians. Females and juveniles are very dark brown, while most males are much paler with silver-grey and russet tones. A small proportion of adult males have plumage that resembles that of the female.

Water Rail *(Rallus aquaticus)*

If you hear the sudden sharp squealing of a pig, coming from deep within a reedbed, it is probably not being made by a pig at all but by a Water Rail. This is

a shy, streaky brown bird with a long red bill, and is related to the much more outgoing Coot and Moorhen. It walks and swims with equal ease, and you are most likely to glimpse it slinking along the reed edge, with head lowered and the short tail raised and constantly flicking. Despite its benign, timid appearance it is an adept predator, hunting small fish and even small birds as well as insects. At some nature reserves it will come and forage underneath bird tables.

Left The Marsh Harrier is a wetland specialist, and on east-coast wetlands in England is the easiest bird of prey to see.

Bearded Tit *(Panurus biarmicus)*

These charming small birds have also benefited from reedbed creation and restoration schemes, but this is tempered by recent losses as a result of the severe winters that ocurred from 2009 to 2013. Bearded Tits are not related to true tits, in fact they have no close relatives anywhere in the world, but do superficially resemble the tits in their agility as they climb through the reed stems. Not particularly timid birds, they are nonetheless often difficult to see, as they keep low (especially on windy days). They are highly sociable and you are likely to encounter them in small parties at all times of the year. In summer they feed on insects, especially the Plum-reed Aphid, but in winter they switch to reed seeds, and to help them digest these they also ingest tiny particles of grit and gravel. At nature reserves, they will visit grit trays provided for them among the reeds. Their preferred habitat is rather exposed and so they can suffer very high mortality in cold winters, but despite their feeble-looking flight they can quickly discover and colonise suitable patches of newly available habitat. When numbers are high, surplus Bearded Tits will disperse in search of new potential breeding grounds and can then turn up in quite small, isolated reedbeds that are many miles from other wetlands.

Reed Warbler (*Acrocephalus scirpaceus*)

The ceaseless, rhythmic song of the Reed Warbler provides an unmistakeable backing track for the reedbed in summer. Seeing the rather plain-looking, milky tea-coloured bird is more of a challenge than hearing it, as it tends to stay well hidden among the stems, but soon after arriving from the African wintering grounds the female Reed Warblers will spend much of their time climbing to the tips of flowering reed stems to collect the fronds for their nests, and then they are easy to observe. This species has increased strongly in England through the 21st century and is spreading in Wales, Ireland and Scotland. Its current 'boom' is helping to mitigate the ongoing decline of the Cuckoo, which in some areas parasitises its nests.

Sedge Warbler (*Acrocephalus schoenobaenus*)

Closely related to the Reed Warbler, the Sedge Warbler occurs in reedbeds but also in slightly drier, more scrubby areas, though still close to water. Its song is similar but more varied and more exciteable-sounding, and it is also a more boldly marked bird and a more showy character, often singing in plain view at the top of a bush,

Far left Bearded Tits are very distinctive and attractive little birds, which depend on reedbed habitats.

Above A male Sedge Warbler performing his spring song-flight.

Left The dead heads of last year's reeds provide perfect nesting material for Reed Warblers.

and sometimes in flight. In early autumn as it prepares to migrate, the Sedge Warbler becomes more strictly a reedbed bird as it fills up on the abundant Plum-reed Aphids, stacking on as much weight as it can to fuel its migration to Africa.

Reed Bunting (*Emberiza schoeniclus*)

The most easily seen small bird of the reeds, the Reed Bunting is a rather sparrow-like little brown bird, though the male in summer is more striking with his black head and white half-collar and moustache. Males are more noticeable than females by their behaviour too – they often choose the tallest reed around and perch at the top of it as they deliver their rather unimpressive brief song. Reed Warblers feed on insects in spring and summer, and switch to seeds in winter. At this time, many of them will disperse away from wetlands and join flocks of finches and other buntings on farmland – they will also visit gardens.

Many other birds make more casual use of reedbeds. In winter, vast flocks of roosting Starlings take shelter in them, and dense reedbeds also provide safe overnight accommodation for flocks of Swallows and martins in autumn, before these birds begin their migration. A rare but regular visitor to Britain, the Penduline Tit, turns up almost exclusively in coastal reedbeds, especially those with a good proportion of Common Reedmace plants. The old, fluffy seed heads of Reedmace attract other birds in spring, as they make superb nest-lining material. Dabbling ducks, Coots

Below

The simple but persistent song of the Reed Bunting is a classic wetland sound.

and Moorhens often nest on dry patches of ground among the reeds, and tend their ducklings in the sheltered channels between reed stands.

DRAGONS AND DAMSELS

Marshlands, creeks and lagoons are home to many insects. They are most in evidence in the summer when the adults are on the wing, but many wetland insects are aquatic in their larval stages (and a few remain water animals as adults) and form an important part of the underwater ecosystem. They provide food for fish, frogs and newts, Water Shrews and birds – some break down dead plants and animals, and some are hunters of other water creatures.

Dragonflies and damselflies, members of the insect order Odonata, are the most striking wetland insects. They are skilled and fearless predators. As underwater larvae, they hunt tiny insects and arthropods, and the larger ones stalk tadpoles, fish fry and other small creatures across the lake bed. When the mature larvae climb up emergent stems of waterside plants and undergo their final transformation, the winged adults turn their predatory talents to the aerial world, catching flying insects smaller and slower than themselves (which, in the case of the largest dragonflies, means all flying insects). Damselflies are quite small and delicate with slim bodies and a fluttering flight. Dragonflies are larger and much more strongly built, with a powerful and direct flight action. They can hover on the spot with ease and even fly backwards – these flying skills are not just

Below A pair of Common Darter dragonflies complete their complex mating ritual.

The dragon and the dragon-slayer

Below The Migrant Hawker dragonfly (right) and the Hobby (left) – two fearsome aerial hunters, but the falcon is the nemesis of the dragon.

One of the most common dragonflies on coastal marshland is the Migrant Hawker, a medium-sized, mostly blue (browner in females) dragon which can be extremely numerous in late summer and early autumn. This species formerly occurred in Britain only as a migrant from further south, but has spread northwards across Britain over the last few decades and now breeds here in high numbers – and it is still a migratory visitor as well.

The spread of the Migrant Hawker is mirrored by that of one of our most impressive birds of prey, the Hobby. This is a small falcon which specialises in catching tricky prey on the wing – including fast-flying birds but also large numbers of insects. They are specialists at catching dragonflies, and are often seen hunting over wetlands. As Migrant Hawkers have expanded their range northwards, so have Hobbies.

The Migrant Hawker is particularly important prey for Hobbies for two key reasons. The first is their abundance. They are less territorial than other large dragonflies, so can exist at very high densities – enough to support plenty of hungry Hobbies. The second is the timing of their flight season – late in the year, at the time when young Hobbies are living independently and feeding up for their first migration, but are not quite the consummate prey-catchers they are destined to become. They are in need of an abundant and reliable food source, and the massed Migrant Hawkers fit the bill. Many coastal marshes are not suitable for Hobbies to nest near as they lack tall trees, but after the breeding season the Hobbies head marsh-wards to exploit the dragon bonanza.

regularly flooded grassland is an important part of coastal wetland habitats. Like open water, it has a natural tendency to dry out over time, and so it is often managed in various ways to prevent this. Using livestock to control the growth of larger plants is the cornerstone of managing wet grassland.

Wet meadowland is a particularly important habitat for nesting waders. Relatively few wader species breed in Britain,

Left Emerald Damselflies are on the wing from July into early autumn.

Below In September, Migrant Hawkers vastly outnumber other dragonflies at wetlands across England.

used for hunting, but in territorial conflicts and in the rather challenging process of mid-air mating.

Not all dragonflies and damselflies can live happily in coastal marshland. Several British species only occur on peat bogs, while others need fast-flowing clean rivers, or freshwater pools free of salinity. The species you are most likely to see around coastal wetlands are those that can, as larvae, live in slightly brackish water. They include Blue-tailed, Emerald and Scarce Emerald Damselflies, and Four-spotted Chaser, Common Darter and Migrant Hawker dragonflies. The Dainty Damselfly, which may now be extinct in Britain, was a coastal marshland specialist when it occurred here, although its habitat preferences are more catholic in mainland Europe.

WET MEADOWS AND MOORS
As well as open water and fringing vegetation, wet and

and even fewer in the lowlands. Three that do are the Lapwing, the Redshank and the Common Snipe. The Lapwing is red-listed as a species of conservation concern, while the other two are both on the amber list, and one of the main problems they face is lack of breeding habitat.

Drainage dries out the meadows, removing the soft muddy patches that wader chicks need to find tiny insects to eat. In winter, grazing marsh often floods and then becomes attractive to flocks of wildfowl, including Bewick's and Whooper Swans, various geese, and Wigeons.

On less fertile soil, wet, boggy moorland is found close to the coast. This habitat is found in more northerly areas, and in summer is home to a range of interesting breeding birds, such as Hen Harrier, Merlin, Short-eared Owl and, at a tiny number of sites, the charming Red-

throated Phalarope, which breeds on small moorland ponds.

Right The Stonechat is one of several heathland and moorland birds that relocate to marshy coasts for the winter.

Far right If you visit the marshy moors of Fetlar in Shetland in summer, you could see Red-throated Phalaropes in their colourful breeding plumage.

THE MARSH THROUGH THE SEASONS

Richly vegetated coastal wetlands hold plenty of interest for the wildlife-watcher all year round. In winter, they can teem with birdlife, and become even busier when inland waters start to freeze up. The birds arrange themselves according to their feeding methods, with small waders keeping to the shores and shallows, while longer-legged species like Avocets and Black-tailed Godwits walk into deeper water and sometimes swim. Dabbling ducks like Teals, Shovelers and Gadwalls also prefer fairly shallow water, but the deepest parts of the lake are used by diving ducks, such as Pochards and Tufted Ducks, and you may find scarcer species among them, such as Goldeneyes, Scaups and Smews. Other deep-water birds include grebes and divers. Occasionally, seaducks such as Long-tailed Duck and Common Scoter will visit deep pools on the coast. Wild geese and swans tend to feed on farmland, but come to coastal wetlands to rest and roost.

Many birds that breed inland on heaths and high moorlands will move down to coastal areas for the winter, to escape the worst of the winter. Check fence posts and the tops of bushes for Stonechats, pert little birds that are nearly always seen in male-female pairs. Coastal populations of Meadow Pipits, Linnets and Skylarks swell in winter as birds from the uplands join the local breeding birds, and

Below Lapwings need wet grassland with boggy spots and small pools to breed successfully.

Marsh Frogs

In Britain, we have six or seven native species of amphibians – three species of newt, two toads, and one or two frogs (there is some uncertainty over whether the rare Pool Frog is native or introduced). The frog that is most likely to be seen – and heard – in marshland on the south-east coast of England is definitely not a native though.

The Marsh Frog is the largest European frog species, with large specimens measuring some 17cm from snout to backside (and much longer if the full stretch of the legs is included. It is variable in colour, some are drab brown and others very bright green. Native to central Europe and Asia, it was introduced to Britain in 1935 by a wealthy couple who lived near Ashford, Kent, who brought a dozen back from Hungary to live in their garden pond. The frogs, however, didn't follow their instructions and promptly left, instead colonising nearby ditches and pools, and quickly spreading in all directions. Today, their chorus of loud laughing croaks form a very obvious part of the southern marshland soundtrack through the warmer months. They are very aquatic frogs, living in the water or just by it all year round, unlike our native Common Frogs which live mainly on land.

There is not yet any conclusive evidence that the presence of these non-native frogs is harmful to marshland ecosystems – it is possible that they could be outcompeting native amphibians. Marsh Frogs do provide (very substantial) meals for predators such as Grey Herons and Grass Snakes.

Below A Marsh Frog shows off its long limbs as it swims down a freshwater ditch.

Wetlands

Water Pipits, which do not breed in Britain, visit in small numbers. Upland birds of prey also arrive, with the likes of Hen Harrier, Merlin and Short-eared Owl all turning up to hunt over rough grazing marshes. The Merlin hunts smaller birds, but the harrier and the owl prefer to take voles, and it is not unusual to see four or five Short-eared Owls quartering over the same field following a good vole summer. In very boggy wet meadows and around reedbed fringes you could find visiting Jack Snipes, and it is easier to see shy Bitterns and Water Rails in the winter months.

As spring arrives, so insects begin to emerge. The first damselfly on the wing is usually the Large Red Damselfly, which occurs throughout the British Isles, and at the same time the less common Hairy Dragonfly begins to appear. Other insects of wetland areas include alderflies, which are plump, slow-moving and carry their lattice-patterned wings in a tent-shape over their bodies – look for them on reed stems and on wooden fences and bridges over streams and ditches. St Mark's Flies are fuzzy black creatures that appear in profusion around St Mark's Day – 25th April – they are an important food source for the first migrant birds to return at the start of the breeding season. In spring you may also be lucky enough to witness freshwater fish such as Pike spawning in shallow water.

Summer-visiting birds start to appear in March, and keep on coming through April and May. Overnight the sky over the wetlands fills with Swifts, Swallows and martins, all taking advantage of mass emergences of mosquitoes and other flying insects before moving on to their breeding grounds. Wetland plants begin to flower, and island lakes begin to fill up with nesting pairs of Black-headed Gulls, Common Terns and Little Ringed Plovers.

Summer is the best season for watching mammals. Water Voles have suffered massive population declines in Britain, partly thanks to the proliferation

Below Black-headed Gulls form large and very loud colonies on coastal marshland.

Overleaf A wetland scene in autumn – hundreds of recently arrived Black-tailed Godwits feed and rest, in company with a few others including Lapwings and Avocets.

Right
Water Voles
are confident
swimmers
and divers.

As autumn progresses, the winter birds of the wetlands – flocks of ducks, geese and waders – begin to arrive. This is also the best time of year to look for scarcer birds. Carefully check any waders you see to look for less common species like Little Stint, Spotted Redshank and Wood Sandpiper – with luck you could even find real rarities like Pectoral Sandpiper. Young birds of many species will be making their first migration through September and October, and can get lost on the way. Coastal headlands are the likeliest places for them to turn up, as they head for the nearest land they can find, and those that

of the non-native American Mink. Efforts to eliminate minks and reintroduce Water Voles have been very successful in some areas, and the natural recovery of the Otter seems to be helping to reduce mink numbers too, as Otters seem to keep minks away, whether through confrontation or simply through out-competing them. Visit the wetlands early in the morning and keep quiet to improve your chances of seeing any of these mammals. Rough grazing pasture is a great habitat for Stoats and Weasels, and also provides breeding ground for waders like Redshanks, Lapwings and Snipes.

Through late summer and early autumn, the waders that breed in the high Arctic begin their southwards migrations, and stop off at coastal marshland,

both salt and freshwater, to feed. The first birds to arrive tend to be adults that did not breed, with the juveniles coming later. Many of the first adult birds will still be in their impressive summer plumage. You could see male Ruffs still sporting their ornate head plumes, beautiful scarlet Curlew Sandpipers and Knots, and Golden Plovers still wearing their bright spangled gold and black finery. Reedbeds will be alive with young warblers and Bearded Tits feasting on Reed-plum Aphids, and the late-season dragonflies such as Migrant Hawker will be out in profusion, along with the Hobbies that hunt them. Ospreys begin to migrate south in August and will stop off at large lakes and harbours, often staying for days or even weeks.

Wetlands

happen to be wetland species will then seek out the nearest marshy area they can find.

PLACES TO VISIT

Here is a selection of the best coastal marshes and wetlands to watch wildlife around the British Isles.

ENGLAND

Rainham Marshes, Greater London

Centuries ago, the tidal Thames would have been lined with wild marshland, but the area is very heavily developed today, thanks to London's eastward sprawl. Rainham Marshes RSPB, on the north shore of the river, is a little oasis among the flyovers, pylons and tower blocks. A couple of decades of careful landscaping work has restored it from neglected MoD land to a complex mix of grazing marsh, lakes, ditches, reedbed and wet woodland. In winter the shallow 'flashes' fill up with Wigeons and other waterfowl, in spring the reedbeds are full of warbler song, and in high summer the reserve is alive with insect life. Nationally scarce species like Marsh Harrier, Bearded Tit, Water Vole and many rare invertebrates occur here, and visitor facilities make it ideal for a family day out.

Above Rainham Marshes in London offers an idea of what the whole tidal Thames area would have been like a few centuries ago.

Left Rare waders may turn up on coastal marshes in autumn – the most frequent transatlantic visitor is the Pectoral Sandpiper.

Oare Marshes, Kent

This is a Kent Wildlife Trust reserve on the southern edge of the Swale, consisting of large lagoons and extensive reedbeds, and patches of wet meadowland. Nature trails circle the eastern lagoon and go along the foreshore of the Swale. Huge flocks of Avocets, Black-tailed Godwits and Golden Plovers visit the lagoon in late summer through to early winter, with many other waders also present in smaller numbers. The birds can be observed at very close quarters from the roadside, while the 'seawatching' hide overlooking the Swale is a great place to watch seabirds like skuas and terns on stormy autumn high tides.

Minsmere, Suffolk

Known to many thanks to its 2014 appearances on the BBC's *Springwatch*, this jewel of an RSPB reserve holds a wide range of habitats, including freshwater lakes, saltmarsh, wet pasture and woodland, as well as the seashore. It is a wonderful place to see Bitterns and Otters, which make regular appearances in front of the Island Mere hide. Avocets breed in good numbers, and many waders visit in autumn and winter. Many rarities have been found on the site. A diverse range of invertebrate life has also been recorded here, including an impressive 24 species of dragonflies and damselflies, and 33 butterflies. A short walk along the beach brings you to Dunwich Heath, a National Trust site comprising coastal heathland, where scarce species such as Dartford Warbler and the Silver-studded Blue butterfly occur.

Below A group of birdwatchers checking out the action at Oare Marshes, Kent.

Wetlands

Titchwell, Norfolk

One of the string of stunning
nature reserves along the north
Norfolk coast, Titchwell RSPB is
enormously popular and with
good reason. There are extensive
reedbeds which support
Bitterns, Marsh Harriers and
Bearded Tits in good numbers,
and open fresh water and
brackish and saltwater
marshland as well. The resident
insects on the reserve are joined
by immigrants from Europe,
including thousands of Painted
Lady and Clouded Yellow
butterflies in favourable years.
There are also many spectacular
flowering plants on the reserve,
including Southern Marsh
Orchids. On the beach, flocks of
Sanderlings, Knots and other
waders can be seen, and often
there are interesting birds going
by offshore, including rafts of

Left A Southern
Marsh Orchid at
Titchwell, Norfolk.

Above The
Silver-studded Blue
butterfly is a rare
and beautiful species
that can be found on
the coastal
heathland near
Minsmere, Suffolk.

Below

The Common Hawker is a large dragonfly with yellow-edged wings and, in the male, a pronounced 'wasp-waist'.

scoters in winter. Close to Titchwell are other wonderful marshlands including Cley Marshes and Stiffkey Marsh.

Marshside, Lancashire

Just down the road from Southport, this RSPB reserve is very easily accessed and has saltmarsh and freshwater marsh, divided by the coast road and overlooked by two birdwatching hides. In winter, huge flocks of Pink-footed Geese arrive here and can be seen resting on the saltmarsh, while in summer Lapwings nest on the wet meadows and Avocets on the pools. Nearby is Leighton Moss RSPB, a marshy area adjacent to Morecambe Bay which has large areas of reedbeds and open water.

Saltholme, County Durham

One of the RSPB's most ambitious projects in recent years, Saltholme is a new wetland reserve created by the tidal River Tees. The site is still in its infancy but already attracts masses of birdlife, including flocks of ducks and waders in autumn and winter, and the list of rarities recorded here is impressive. Water Voles are thriving here, and the dragonfly pools have produced sightings of many species, including the (actually not very common) Common Hawker.

WALES

Newport Wetlands, Newport County

Wales as a country has a mostly rocky shoreline with relatively

few sizeable marshy areas, which makes this wetland site – an NNR, SPA and SAC as well as an RSPB reserve – extra important. The reedbeds have attracted both Marsh Harriers and Bitterns, both very scarce in Wales, and in 2014 the usual reedbed warblers were joined by a singing Savi's Warbler, a very rare bird which only sporadically breeds in Britain. Otters are seen regularly all year round, the site teems with insect life in summer, and in winter the reedbeds sometimes play host to a spectacularly large roost of Starlings.

SCOTLAND

Loch Gruinart, Argyll

The island of Islay is beautiful and, mostly, steep and rugged. In the north-west lies this RSPB reserve, an area of low-lying wet meadowland adjoining a sea loch, and it is a magical place to watch wildlife. In winter, thousands of Barnacle and White-fronted Geese arrive to feed on the meadowland, while in early summer this is a place to see one of Britain's most beautiful and scarce butterflies, the Marsh Fritillary. Otters are commonly seen, and even Golden Eagles sometimes wander over from the hillier parts of the island.

Hobbister, Orkney

The 70 or so islands that make up Orkney offer amazing wildlife-watching across a remarkable variety of habitats – some islands are rugged with steep cliff coasts, others low-lying and richly vegetated. The RSPB reserve of Hobbister is on Mainland, the largest island, and has areas of saltmarsh and boggy coastal moorland with breeding Twites, Hen Harriers, Short-eared Owls, Merlins and, on the small lochans, Red-throated Divers. It also offers other habitats to explore – it overlooks the deep waters of Scapa Flow, where seabirds and cetaceans may be seen.

IRELAND

Wexford Wildfowl Reserve, Co Wexford

This lively nature reserve is designated an SPA and a Ramsar site, as well as an NNR. Overlooking Wexford Harbour, it is made up of shallow marshy lakes and wet grassland, and is an important wintering site for White-fronted Geese and Brent Geese. It also attracts Whooper and Bewick's Swans along with a range of ducks, including several stray North American vagrants. The harbour is also important for wading birds, and the area has racked up an astonishing total of 42 species over the years. Irish Hares can be found in the grassy areas, and Grey and Common Seals haul out on sandbanks in the harbour mouth.

Tacumshin Lake, Co Wexford

This coastal lagoon is near-legendary among birdwatchers, with an impressive record for attracting vagrant North American species. Pectoral, White-rumped, Baird's and Buff-breasted Sandpipers occcur every autumn, and rarer species are found in most years. The lake has breeding Shelducks and Water Rails, and on spring migration Little Gulls are regularly seen.

Top Savi's Warbler is one of the rarest British wetland warblers

Above The Whooper Swans that visit us in winter are mainly Icelandic breeding birds.

Loch Gruinart, on Islay.

Rocks

Rocky shorelines, too low or too gradually sloped to be defined as cliff-faces, are common in the north and west of the British Isles. However, outcrops of solid rock are a feature of many flatter beaches in southern and eastern areas. There are also 'boulder beaches', made of loose, large chunks of rock. All have in common the fact that their substrate is not mobile, unlike the smaller particles that make up sand or shingle beaches. Therefore, rocks provide a solid mooring for sea animals. Some of these can withstand periodic exposure to the air, on the low tides, while others stay immersed in water permanently by inhabiting rock pools. Shorelines of this kind are fascinating places to explore, with 'rockpooling' something of a national pastime.

WHERE ROCKS STAND

Only hard rock, such as limestone, can endure the constant battering of the sea year after year. Softer, sedimentary rock like sandstone is quickly worn away and the resulting sediment carried in the sea, to be deposited in places where the sea action is calm enough to allow it to settle out. In places where the coast is exposed to strong wave action, the shoreline tends to be rocky, with beaches only forming in sheltered cracks and coves.

Like beaches, rocky shores have distinct zonation, according to how much of the time they are covered by sea water. Above the high water mark is the supratidal zone, also known as the 'splash zone'. This area only receives sporadic dousing with seawater, from wave splashes, and on occasion from storm-surge tides. Closer to the sea is the intertidal zone, which is regularly covered by the incoming tide, and this can be further divided into three sub-zones – the high tide/high intertidal zone, which is covered at high tide only, the middle tide zone/mid-littoral zone which is covered about half the time, and finally the low intertidal zone/lower littoral zone, which is only exposed at low tide. On steep shores, the zones may be very narrow, but each zone still supports a distinct range of organisms (as well as others that are versatile enough to live in all zones).

Rock pools are hollows in the surfaces of the rocks that trap sea water when the tide retreats. The kinds of plants that grow and animals that live in rock pools varies according to which zone the pool is in, and how deep it is. The water in rock pools is stirred up and replaced every time the tide covers it, so free-living rock pool inhabitants may only be temporary residents, while those that live anchored to the rock in

Below 'Shelves' of sedimentary rock on the coast of northern Northumberland.

some way are permanent (or at least more permanent, but have to endure quite turbulent conditions when the pool is covered.

ANIMALS OF THE ROCKPOOLS

Exploring rockpools is one of the great joys of a seaside visit. These tiny pockets of trapped sea water offer a challenging environment – sometimes the water in them is part of the moving sea, swirling and stirring about in turbulent conditions, and sometimes it is completely still and warming up quickly under the power of the sun – or being diluted by falling rain. Nevertheless, a wonderful variety of animals can be found in rockpools.

Sea anemones These beautiful, flower-like animals belong to a phylum called Cnidaria, sometimes known as 'polyps'. They are related to the free-swimming jellyfish – both sea anemones and jellyfish use stinging tentacles to catch their prey, subdue it with stings and paralysing venom, and bring it to their mouths. An 'open' anemone shows a mass of soft, waving tentacles protruding from its squat base, which is anchored firmly to the rock. Anything mobile may be caught, especially tiny fish and shrimps, but also drifting bits of carrion. When it has caught prey, in most species the tentacles are drawn in and the anemone becomes a jelly-like blob – it also goes into 'blob mode' when its rock pool is drying out or becoming too warm under the sunshine. These animals can reproduce asexually, by 'budding' miniature versions of themselves. They can move but do so only slowly and reluctantly. Occasionally, an anemone attaches itself to a crab's carapace, and both crab and anemone benefit – the crab from a stinging protector, the anemone from food particles floating its way as the crab feeds. The small, red Beadlet Anemone is our commonest species. A larger but shorter-bodied species, with a more open 'face' and relatively short tentacles is the Dahlia Anenome. On western coasts, in rock pools near the low water mark, you may find the striking green-tentacled Snakelocks Anemone, which as its name suggests possesses a luxuriant 'head' of long, flowing tentacles. Our prettiest species is probably the Jewel Anemone, a rather scarce species found in deep, shaded rockpools. Its body and tentacles sport bright tones of green, violet and yellow.

Crabs Finding a crab is a treat for the rockpooler, as these

Top left The Beadlet Anemone is a small species with rather short tentacles.

Bottom left Exposed to the air, a Beadlet Anemone withdraws its tentacles and turns into a blob of jelly.

Above The Shore Crab is our most common crab species, and may be seen around freshwater coastal pools as well as rockpools.

Right Through its life, a Hermit Crab may occupy the empty shells of several different gastropod species.

crustaceans are fascinating to observe close up, but be careful not to get pinched – if you are going to pick one up, take hold of it gently and carefully with your thumb and forefinger at the sides of its carapace. Crabs have 10 legs, the front pair of which bear the claws, stalked eyes, and short antennae. The crabs you find in rock pools tend to be small, immature individuals that can shelter under objects in the pool – full-grown crabs require more spacious accommodation. Crabs grow through successive moults – the emerging animal is soft-bodied and will expand in size before its body hardens. The

moult also allows the crab to regrow any limbs that it may have lost. The Shore Crab is our most common species and in its immature stages can be strikingly coloured and patterned in greens, greys and white. Adults are a dark, drab brown. The Common Hermit Crab lacks a hard carapace, instead using an empty gastropod mollusc shell into which it winds its soft, elongated body, tucking its legs out of sight inside the shell mouth if necessary. As it grows, it needs to find replacement shells. Hermit crabs are easily distinguished from the actual molluscs whose shells they use by the speed at which they move – a nippy crab scuttle rather than a slow snail slide.

Shrimps and prawns Part of the same taxomonic order as crabs, these animals look superficially quite unlike crabs but the differences are mainly a matter of relative proportions and shapes. Shrimps and prawns are also 10-legged, with small claws on the front pair. They have antennae (much longer than those of crabs) and stalked eyes, and have a carapace over the front of their bodies. The abdomen, which in crabs is short and tucked under the carapace, is elongated in shrimps and prawns, and bears 'pleopods' – swimming legs. Like crabs, they are predators and scavengers, but get about more by swimming than by walking (although they can do both). The Common Prawn often uses rockpools in its early life – it is difficult to spot, being almost translucent, but wait patiently and you may see it dart across an

open part of the water. The Snakelocks Shrimp is a beautiful, colourful and rare animal with blue spots on its delicate, transparent body. It lives in symbiosis with the Snakelocks Anemone, in a similar arrangement to the much more famous association between clownfish and anemones in the tropics. The Common Lobster, big brother to the shrimps and prawns, sometimes occurs in rockpools when immature. Young lobsters lack the deep blue colouration of mature individuals but have the same large claws and 'fantail'.

Fish As with crabs and other mobile crustaceans, the fish that you might find in rockpools are sometimes temporary residents, the young of more wide-ranging marine fish, with the chance of being moved on by the next incoming tide. However, some species are well adapted to live long-term in rockpools as long

Above A Common Lobster shows off its formidable armoury.

Left Beautifully camouflaged, the Rock Goby waits motionless for prey to happen along.

as there is enough space for them to hide and to hunt. The kinds of fish that occur in rockpools are species that are not restlessly active but happy to lurk in hidden spots and wait for the opportunity to catch passing prey. The Rock Goby rests on top of rocks in pools, and its fused pelvic fins function as a sort of sucker, helping it to hold its position. It is a pretty, dappled fish with large fins and its eyes set high on its head. The Common Blenny is one of several species of blenny that may be found in rockpools; it has a tapered shape and its dorsal fin runs along its full body length.

This fish often stays in the same rockpool for many weeks or months. The Long-spined Sea Scorpion or Long-spined Bullhead is a large-headed fish with extravagantly large, spined pectoral fins. It uses its mottled rock-like colouring to stay hidden in plain sight as it waits for prey to wander by. It then uses its large extendible mouth to suck up its victims. The slippery Butterfish is an eel-like creature with small fins (only the low dorsal fin and small pectoral fins are evident) and a row of black spots down its back. Sticklebacks are thought of as freshwater fishes but can

actually live quite happily in saltwater; the slim-bodied Fifteen-spined Stickleback can be found in rockpools around the British Isles.

Starfish and sea urchins These animals belong to the phylum Echinodermata, which means 'hedgehog skin' and aptly describes their spiny appearance. Both are symmetrical animals, but starfish have more mobile, softer bodies and a variable number of arms, while sea urchins look like solid spheres covered with long spines. Some are vegetarian, eating algae and seaweed, while

Below This sea urchin's spiny coat wasn't enough to protect it from a hungry Otter.

others are carnivorous or scavenge dead organic material. The Cushion Star is a small, pale and plump starfish with five quite short arms. It has the interesting quirk of changing sex after its first four years of life, from male to female – if you find one larger than 2cm across it is probably a female. Sunstars are also plump-bodied, but much larger and have up to 14 arms. The long-armed Spiny Starfish may be found in rockpools near the low water mark. It has a small body and five long arms with obvious stout spikes, and can reach a diameter of 70cm. Good-sized specimens of the Common Starfish are often found dead in the strandline, but small ones may live in rockpools. This five-armed starfish, which reaches 50cm across, preys on mussels, prising the mollusc's valves apart before everting their stomach directly into the opened shell to digest its contents. Brittlestars have even longer and slimmer arms, which come off when the animal is under attack, and can be regrown. The Green Sea Urchin is our most familiar species of urchin, and has a round body in five 'segments', though these are not obvious in a living individual. It is a small urchin (up to 5cm across) and feeds mainly on seaweeds. After death, the spines are lost leaving a round empty shell or 'test', with a hole in its centre and a dense covering of wart-like bumps which mark where the spines had been eaten by Otter

Protecting rockpool life

When you investigate rockpools, it is important to remember that many of the animals living in them are very fragile, and some have permanent residences among the stones and other material on the bed of the pool. Handle both the animals and their environment with great care to ensure you cause no harm. If moving a stone to see what's underneath, lift it gently and replace it as close to its exact original position as you can. When you look at animals, they will be more comfortable if you place them in a receptacle (a small white plastic pot is fine) with a little water rather than hold them in your hand. Be careful not to mix several animals in the same container in case one is a predator of another. You may find you see more life and activity if you don't disturb the water at all but just watch – make sure your shadow does not fall on the water as this often triggers animals to rush for shelter. And finally, resist the temptation to bring rockpool animals home. Keeping them alive and happy in a home environment is extremely difficult, even for experts, so just enjoy watching them in their natural habitat.

Below Every rockpool is a complete ecosystem in miniature, and should be treated with care and respect.

A sheltered cove with rocky edges such as here at Lulworth Cove in Dorset, offers fantastic potential for discovering all kinds of marine life.

Right The hole in the top of the Acorn Barnacle at the front centre of this group shows that the animal itself has died, but its outer plates remain intact.

Below 'Settled' adult barnacles continue to grow, by adding new layers to the calcified plates that surround them.

Odds and ends Other animals you may find in rockpools include mussels and periwinkles, marine worms, Sea Hares, which are shell-less gastropods, and chitons, which are molluscs but look like leg-less woodlice, with a row of hard plates rather than a single shell or pair of valves. One of the most stunning and un-animal-like animals of the rockpool is the rare Star Ascidian, a colonial tunicate or sea-squirt, which forms a jelly-like mat, marked with regular flower-like patterns.

BLISTERING BARNACLES

Rocks that are sea-covered for at least half the time are likely to bear a white crust of barnacles. The same goes for artificial structures like breakwaters, and even limpets, mussels and other more or less stationary animals often have barnacles on board as well. Because the barnacles we see are non-moving, we often assume they are molluscs, perhaps miniature cousins of the similarly static and rock-clinging limpets, but in fact they are crustaceans, related to crabs, lobsters and other very mobile marine animals.

Barnacles don't spend their entire lives fixed to the spot. In their youth they are free-wheeling (or free-drifting, at least), and are part of the zooplankton that is such an important component of marine ecosystems. The first larval lifestage of a barnacle is called a nauplius – it has long, freely moving limbs for swimming. At the next lifestage, the larva is known as a cyprid. The barnacle is now ready – literally – to settle down. It does not feed but moves about in search of a suitable place to spend the rest of its life, and when it finds somewhere that feels like home it fixes itself in place by secreting a cement-like substance. Once fixed, it moults into its final adult form, and generates its hard, protective plates. It is able to close its soft feeding appendages behind a 'trapdoor' between these plates when exposed to the air, protecting its body from drying out.

When underwater, barnacles open up their 'trapdoors' and extend their cirri or feeding legs into the water to trap particles of food. The cirri are elegant long feathery structures, but they are not the most impressive appendages that barnacles possess. These animals need to reach each other in order to reproduce, but being fixed to the spot can make this difficult. To overcome the challenge, barnacles possess what are

proportionately the longest penises in the animal world – eight times longer than the width of the barnacle itself. With this impressive organ, a barnacle reaches across to its nearest neighbour in order to mate – because barnacles are (usually) hermaphrodite, there is no need for discrimination.

The Acorn Barnacle is by far the most common and familiar species, producing the characteristic white crust on every static surface that lies below the mid-shore. Other British species include the darker Montagu's Barnacle, found higher up on the shore, the tall-shelled Volcano Barnacle of south-west England and Wales, and the very rare and very striking, Goose-necked Barnacle, a large, complex-looking barnacle with a mosaic-like appearnce to its shell. It is fixed to its rock by a stalk – its 'goose-neck'. Despite its

impressive appearance it has been found to be poorly endowed in the penis department for a barnacle, its appendage a mere two-thirds of its body length, but it reproduces by 'sperm-casting' – releasing sperm into the water for others to capture, rather than directly into a neighbour's shell.

THE SEASIDE SONGBIRD

Birdwatchers coming to the seaside know that most of the birds they see will be larger species – waders, gulls, cormorants and the like. The shore is not a very hospitable environment for 'little birds' to live and breed, as they really need to have their nest site close to their feeding grounds. In winter, some small birds do spend time on the coast – Snow Buntings and Shore Larks come and feed on the strandline and around plants above the high water mark, and they may be joined by the likes of Pied

Below

Goosenecked Barnacles are very striking and it is clear from this picture why they are so named with shells that almost resemble goose heads.

Right Rock Pipits have a much duskier appearance than the other common British pipit species.

Below Because there are few predators of small songbirds on rocky coasts, this Rock Pipit can feed its chick out in the open.

Wagtails, Linnets and Meadow Pipits. In summer, Swallows and martins may hunt over the beach, although they tend to find more of their preferred prey (flying insects) inland. But there is one small bird that you will find on rocky coastlines all year round.

The Rock Pipit is not a very striking bird, and is probably overlooked by many visitors to the coast. A little larger than a House Sparrow, it is dark brown above with heavy dusky streaking on its paler belly, but no really noticeable markings. However, it has a lively, inquisitive and assertive character, and is a real pleasure to watch as it goes about its business marching about on and around the rocks in search of insects, sandhoppers and tiny crustaceans, and going back and forth to its nest, tucked in the hollow of a sea cave or similar sheltered spot. In spring and summer, the males can be seen performing their songflight, which involves a steep climb followed by descending 'parachute-style' on partly opened wings. In some parts of the country, the Rock Pipit is an important host of Cuckoos, and because Rock Pipits are by nature bold and approachable and will feed their fledged chicks out in the open, this can be an amazing opportunity to watch the host-Cuckoo relationship at close quarters.

Rock Pipits are scarce on flatter coastlines but wherever there are rocks or cliffs you will find them. In towns and villages on suitable coasts, they will even nest in crevices in buildings, and may forage for crumbs on roads and pavements. Most of our breeding birds stay put on their territories all year, but the most northerly birds are partly migratory, and they do visit a wider range of habitats in winter. Some of the birds here in winter are not residents but visitors from Scandinavia. They are of a different subspecies (our resident form is *Anthus petrosus petrosus*, while the Scandinavian birds are *Anthus petrosus littoralis*). The *littoralis* birds are paler in colour, and closer in appearance to the closely related Water Pipit.

Rockpool margins offer feeding opportunities for Rock Pipits all year round.

Right Dense seaweed growth in rockpools offers shelter for a range of small animals.

Centre When the sea retreats, seaweeds hang limp, lacking the rigidity that land plants possess.

Below Most green seaweeds have a woolly or feathery texture, while brown and red seaweeds are more structured.

SEAWEED

Seaweeds occur in all our seas, but they need to attach themselves to something solid, and so rocky shores are the best places to find living seaweeds rather than washed-up strandline remains. Seaweeds are simple plants – algae to be exact – but come in a great array of shapes and growth forms. Some are ribbon-like or hair-like, some have many branches, and some have air bladders to give them buoyancy when underwater. Exposed at low tide, they lie flat on the rocks, but when the water is over them they stand tall and, if you are snorkelling over them, or looking into a deep rockpool, the carpet of waving fronds has the

appearance of a lush undersea forest. They shelter and nourish a huge range of animal life, and in some areas are an important food source for people too.

Seaweeds come in three colours – red, green and brown, each group having its own distinct ecology. All gain energy through photosynthesis, the red and brown forms using the light wavelengths that reach them most effectively at their various growth depths. They have gripping 'holdfasts' to anchor them to rocks, but lack roots, instead obtaining the nutrients they need from the sea water around them. Their reproduction can be a complex process – in the case of the brown 'wrack' seaweeds, the same plants produce male and female gametes (single cells, the equivalent of sperm and egg) and release them from specific 'fruiting bodies' into the sea where they mingle and fuse to form free-drifting zygotes, that then settle onto the rocks and begin to grow.

In and around rockpools, you may find the delicate, tissue-like green *Ulva* seaweeds or 'sea lettuces', which become a slimy green homogenous layer when exposed to the air. Rockpools are also home to the beautiful red *Corallina* species, which has slim, many-branched fronds. Oarweed, the main component of 'kelp forest', is a branched brown seaweed with long, ribbon-like fronds. One of the most attractive animals that lives in kelp forest is the striking Blue-rayed Limpet, an oval limpet with electric-blue lines on its shell. Several species of brown seaweed have air bladders, and the commonest is the familar Bladder Wrack, with pairs of rather small bladders along its rather thick fronds. The Egg Wrack has much larger, single bladders, while Channelled Wrack does not have bladders but develops swollen tips to its fronds when it is fruiting.

HAMMER AND TONGS

If you've ever tried to pull a limpet off a rock, you'll know just how firmly these molluscs anchor themselves in place. A 'relaxed' limpet has a pretty firm grasp of its rock, through the suction of its large 'foot', but this grip tightens instantly if the limpet feels any pulling force. This, together with its tapered shape, helps it resist the motion of a rough sea, and also the efforts of predators to dislodge it. However, it's very rare to find an animal in nature that has a foolproof defence against all predators, and the limpet is no exception.

The Oystercatcher is an unmistakable largish wading bird, with its bold black-and-white plumage, long stout orange bill and pink legs. It visits all kinds of shorelines but is the wader most likely to be seen walking about on rocks, especially in winter – only the Turnstone and the Purple Sandpiper have a comparable affinity with rocky shorelines. Oystercatchers are versatile predators as a group, but less so on an individual level. Studies have found that individuals that feed on soft shorelines have more pointed bill shapes that those that mainly take mussels

Below
Oystercatchers can be seen foraging on rocks at the sea edge all year round.

on rocky shores. Of the mussel-feeders, young birds tend to open mussels along the line where the valves meet, using a 'stab and prise' technique, but some adult Oystercatchers, especially males, develop particularly blunt tips to their bills, and use a more brutal hammering technique to smash straight through the side of the shell and gain access to the mussel's flesh.

Some Oystercatchers are also adept at taking limpets; they dislodge the shells with quick, hard pecks where the shell meets rock, and flip the limpet over to eat the flesh. Their attacks are more successful against single limpets than those that are part of a close-knit cluster. So limpets do have some ability to protect themselves from Oystercatchers – stick close to other limpets.

Another adaptation that Oystercatchers have is the way they care for their young. Wader chicks are precocial – able to run about and peck at food as soon as they hatch. This is a good tactic for any birds that nest on the ground, as the chicks would be vulnerable to mammalian predators if stuck helpless in a nest. However, it does depend on a chick-friendly food source nearby, as it is a few weeks before the young birds' wing feathers are developed enough for flight. Adult Oystercatchers, though, bring food to their chicks, placing worms and other prey on the ground for the young to eat. This allows them to nest on tiny islands that are safe from predators, even if those islands have next to no suitable 'native' prey on them – the adults just fly to good feeding grounds and bring home what they find.

PLACES TO VISIT

Here is a selection of the best rocky shorelines to go rockpooling and to watch wildlife around the British Isles.

ENGLAND

Mousehole to Newlyn, Cornwall
Most of the Cornish coastline is rocky, and offers wonderful

Below
The Oystercatcher is an unmistakable bird that occurs along coasts everywhere in Britain.

wildlife-watching and rockpooling. This stretch on the south-western tip can be walked at shore level along some of its length and has some fine rockpools. Near Mousehole a tidal lido is a lovely place to relax and watch for passing seabirds, as well as observe animal life in what amounts to a very large rockpool. Rock Pipits are joined by Black Redstarts in winter, and offshore you can see Grey Seals and, in winter especially, a good range of seabirds close inshore, including Great Northern Divers.

Kimmeridge Bay, Dorset
For the full educational experience, a visit to the Dorset Wildlife Trust's Marine Centre has all the information you need

Above The lido at Mousehole, Cornwall, is a tidal swimming pool, offering sheltered bathing on a rough stretch of coast.

Left An Oystercatcher uses its bill to prise apart the two valves of a mussel.

Large loose boulders can be stable enough to provide homes for seaweeds and sessile animals, though rough seas may shift them about and crush their inhabitants.

Above **The rocky shore at the mouth of the Cuckmere, in East Sussex, offers lovely views across to the Seven Sisters chalk cliffs.**

Right **On the higher, vegetated slopes of rocky shores, above the reach of the tide, look out for Thrift flowers in summer.**

about this exceptional rockpooling site in Purbeck, where at low tide you can explore the pools for a good three hours. The centre also sells equipment, including lines and bait suitable for luring crabs and rockpool fish out of hiding (with no hooks, so no risk of accidentally harming the animals).

Bembridge Ledges, Isle of Wight
A superb place for safe rockpooling, this proposed Marine Conservation Zone lies at the eastern tip of the Isle of Wight. There is a shingle beach here but at low tide, the level rocky platform of 'the Ledge' is revealed. Its rockpools are rich with life, including brittlestars and occasionally even seahorses.

Rocks

Seven Sisters, East Sussex

The stunning white chalk cliffs of the Seven Sisters and, beyond them, Beachy Head, overlook the eastern edge of this lovely shore around the mouth of the river Cuckmere, while the impressive Seaford Head lies to the west. This is probably the most unspoilt estuary on the south coast, and sits within a Country Park that has much to offer the interested wildlife-watcher, including scarce butterflies, nesting Sand Martins, and a range of chalk downland flowers. There is a shingle beach and, at low tide, expanses of seaweed-covered rocks, with rockpools that contain the full range of common rockpool plants and animals.

West Runton, Norfolk

Just east of Cromer on the north-east Norfolk coast, this is a sandy beach which sits at the base of low, crumbly sandstone cliffs, and the rocky outcrops on the shore are great for looking for rockpool wildlife, as well as passing birdlife. The Norfolk Wildlife Trust holds a number of family rockpooling events here, with experts close at hand to help you find the most interesting wildlife and identify anything unusual. This is also a productive area for fossil-hunters, and is famous for the discovery of an almost complete Steppe Mammoth skeleton in the cliffside, which was revealed after erosion from storms in the 1990s.

Left The Purple Sandpiper is a classic bird of rocky shorelines, and is widespread in the winter particularly.

Cresswell Foreshore, Northumberland

This sandy and rocky shoreline is a Wildlife Trust reserve, and the unusual wave-cut platform of rock with its array of shallow pools has an extraordinarily rich resident flora and fauna, including five species of crabs, Butterfish and a diversity of attractive seaweeds. Rockpooling events are held by the Trust in August. Winter is the best time to look for birds like Purple Sandpipers foraging on the rocks, and other waders on the sand.

WALES

Porth y Pwll, Anglesey

One of several attractive rock-lined bays along this stretch of coastline, Porth y Pwll has many large, deep rockpools that are home to the likes of Squat Lobsters, Cushion Stars, Sunstars and the dazzling Blue-rayed Limpet. Rockpooling events are sometimes held here.

SCOTLAND

Killiedraught Bay, Borders

The superb rockpools at this bay hold wildlife like the Breadcrumb Sponge, the extraordinary Bootlace Worm which can grow to well in excess of 15m long, and the lovely Butterfish. As well as being one of the premier rockpooling sites in the whole of Scotland, this is also a wonderful place to watch seabirds from the shore in summer, as the auks, Kittiwakes and Shags that nest at

Right Shags are often thought of as cliff-face birds but will also nest on low rocky coasts.

Far right One of our prettiest molluscs, the Blue-rayed Limpet can be found at Porth y Pwll.

Opposite The rugged west Highlands coast provides great opportunities to watch Otters fishing in the sea.

nearby St Abbs Head regularly fly to and fro, collecting food for their chicks.

Aultbea/Mellon Charles, Highland

The remote and rugged coast of the north-western Highlands is wonderful for wildlife-watching of all kinds. The rocky shores here are not very accessible, but this, together with the lack of regular disturbance means that you can see and get close to a range of wildlife. On the falling tide, look out for Otters hunting through the kelp forests, and you will also see Ringed Plovers and Rock Pipits, with a chance of rarer birds including White-tailed Eagle overhead. In sheltered inlets, Red-throated Divers will be hunting for fish, before flying back inland to their nesting lochans with their catches.

Rocks

IRELAND

Dunseverick Harbour, Co Antrim

This very special harbour has natural rockpools large and deep enough for swimming. If you decide to join the wildlife in the water, bring a mask and snorkel so you can watch the natural world below you at leisure. Unusual species include the China Limpet and Needle Whelk, and Sea Hares gliding though the masses of seaweeds. Nearby is the Giant's Causeway, an amazing mass of naturally formed geometric basalt columns, which holds an array of unusual plantlife.

Cliffs

& headlands

So far we have looked at coasts where the land slopes gradually towards the sea. Cliff coasts are a dramatic contrast, the land looking as though its edges have been abruptly snapped off, leaving a near-vertical face of bare rock. This is not an easy environment for animals to live on, as there is little vegetation, and soft rock is highly likely to crumble and fall away. Yet cliff-faces can hold wildlife at mind-boggling densities – the great 'seabird cities' of cliff-nesting auks, Kittiwakes and other species are among the most impressive natural wildlife spectacles you'll find in Britain, and are of great ecological importance on a world scale. The tops of cliffs are also interesting environments in their own right, particularly in terms of the flowers and invertebrates they support. Coastal headlands, which may or may not have cliff-faces, are of interest to those wanting to see scarce migrant birds, because they project out into the sea and offer first landfall to lost travellers.

BREAKING WAVES

Cliff coasts are found in places where the sea erodes, rather than deposits material. The action of the sea on the lowest part of the land creates a wave-cut notch – a hollowed-out band, over which a shelf of uneroded land hangs. Eventually this unsupported higher rock collapses down into the sea, and the cliff-face retreats, while the sea moves away the fallen rubble and continues to work away at the cliff base. This process happens more quickly where the rock is soft – these cliffs have relatively frequent rockfalls, and their slopes are usually not as

Right
A wave-cut platform or terrace at the foot of a cliff.

Below Sea stacks and arches form as the sea erodes rock of mixed composition at different rates.

steep as those made of harder rock. Wearing of the higher parts of the cliff-face by weather action also contributes to shaping the cliff-face. At low tide, a flat terrace of rock near the waterline may be revealed – this is a wave-cut platform.

Eventually, as the profile of the coastline changes, some coasts backed by cliffs will become sites of deposition rather than erosion, and a beach will build and grow at the base of the cliff. This will eventually lead to the cliff being well separated from the sea. A good example of this can be seen in the town of Hastings in East Sussex, where the old sandstone cliffs that form the 'West Hill' are now separated from the sea by a broad swathe of shingle beach which is still growing because of longshore drift, plus a main road and a strip of beachfront attractions. Further east the gap between beach and cliff becomes much narrower, and beyond the eastern edge of the town the cliffs are still in contact with the sea. Cliffs that are no longer actively being eroded by sea action are called 'dead cliffs', while those that are still in contact with the waves are 'living cliffs' – but these terms don't have any bearing on whether or not the cliff supports wildlife. 'Dead cliffs' are still subject to weathering and may experience rockfalls.

The rock that forms cliffs is not necessarily of a uniform type, and where softer and harder rock types are mixed together some interesting cliff features can result, as the softer rock wears away more quickly than the hard. Headlands tend to be of hard rock, the softer rock around them having worn away. Smaller features include caves, arches, and isolated columns or stacks. These sea stacks are particularly valuable nesting habitat for seabirds, as their separation from the mainland makes them even safer than mainland cliffs from marauding mammalian predators. Seabirds are highly vulnerable to opportunistic mammals like rats, and on the mainland are most likely to be found on the taller, steeper cliffs as these offer the best protection. On mammal-free islands, lower and more gently sloped cliffs will also be colonised by seabirds.

COMMUNITY LIVING

Many of our familiar garden birds have the same basic way of managing their living space in the breeding season. Each pair claims and defends a territory, and this patch of land meets all their needs – it includes food supplies, a choice of nest sites, drinking and bathing water, and places to sleep, sunbathe and shelter from danger or bad

Guillemots are highly gregarious when nesting, as each pair only needs a small area of cliff-ledge.

Right A few Guillemots have white 'spectacle' markings. This 'bridled' form is more common in the north.

weather. Other birds of the same species know where the territory's boundaries are because one or both of the resident pair advertise them with song, and if they invade it away they will be chased out.

Clearly such a strategy couldn't work for seabirds. For a start, the nest has to be on land but food has to be found at sea. And the food that seabirds eat is highly mobile and distributed over a huge area – much too large for any individual bird to defend against other birds. Besides, when multiple birds attack the same panicked shoal of fish, this can improve each individual's chances of success.

Because most songbirds are territorial rather than social in the breeding season, a pair can select the most discreet spot for their nest, and with only two birds visiting the nest, they stand a fair chance of not giving away its location to predators. On a cliff ledge, though, it is not so easy to find a hidden spot, and near-impossible to approach the cliff in a secretive way. If a nest cannot be hidden by conventional means, then an alternative line of defence is to hide it in a crowd. Almost all the nesting spots of a seabird colony are in plain sight, but they are so numerous that each individual nest has a low chance of being targeted, and if it is, then all the neighbouring birds will respond to the danger, making the predator's task much more difficult.

So our cliff-nesting seabirds are highly gregarious at their nest sites, and highly tolerant of each other when at sea looking for food. They are, though still territorial and defend a small area immediately around their nests. The territory might be tiny, but it is still valuable real estate and is defended with vigour, from both the neighbouring adults and from any mobile youngsters that happen to stumble over the boundary. So when you are watching seabirds at their colonies you will probably see plenty of low-key squabbling – for all their general acceptance of community living, each is still very much motivated by self-interest.

Cliffs & headlands

SEABIRDS OF THE CLIFFS

These are the seabird species you are most likely to find breeding on cliff-faces and clifftops.

Guillemot *Uria aalge*

The Guillemot is usually the most numerous auk at any seabird colony. Sleek and upright with chocolate-brown upperparts and a white belly, the Guillemot has a smoothly tapering dagger of a bill, the most obvious distinction between it and the more heavily equipped Razorbill. Guillemots can nest on very narrow ledges – they make no nest but their pyriform (top-shaped) eggs are inclined to spin on the spot if nudged, rather than rolling over the cliffs to their doom. When collecting food for its chick the adult Guillemot brings fish back to the nest singly, held neatly longways and tail-first in the bill. Each pair rears a single chick, which is able to leap into the sea when barely half-grown, and swims out to deeper, safer water under the close care of its father. A small proportion of birds (more further north) have bold white 'spectacles' and are known as 'bridled' Guillemots. In winter, the throat and lower half of the face become white. Guillemots can be found on cliffs around most northern and western coasts of the British Isles, and when not at their nests will spend much time on the sea in large 'rafts'.

Razorbill *Alca torda*

Distinguished from the Guillemot by its vertically flattened, white-banded bill, the Razorbill has a generally squarer, 'blockier' look than the Guillemot even at a distance, and its upperparts are several shades closer to pure black. It looks if anything even more ungainly than the Guillemot on land and especially in flight, its short narrow wings working very hard to lift its portly frame. On and in the water, though, it is very comfortable, and can dive to below 100 metres in its pursuit of fish prey. Razorbills use broader ledges than Guillemots and nest in lower densities – at most colonies Guillemots heavily outnumber them. After breeding,

Below The wings of the Guillemot are adapted for underwater propulsion, but are still (just about) up to the task of flight.

Above Another heavy-bodied, small-winged auk, the Razorbill has a unique head profile.

Right Puffins are frequently assaulted by other seabirds when bringing fish to the nest, so carry as much as they can every time.

they leave the colonies (the youngsters travelling with their fathers) and spend the winter living at sea, though they can often be found quite close inshore. Like Guillemots, they develop white throats and chins in winter.

Puffin *Fratercula arctica*

Our smallest breeding auk is universally recognisable with its clown-face and parrot-beak, even though many people have never seen one in the flesh. Despite its top-heavy look it is much more agile, both in flight and on the ground, than the Guillemot and Razorbill. It nests

Cliffs & headlands

in burrows in soft ground on cliff-tops, sometimes self-dug and sometimes appropriated from Rabbits, and this habit helps protect its single chick or 'puffling' to avoid the attentions of skuas and larger gulls. The adults, though, often run the gauntlet of attack from these birds when flying to the burrow with a billful of food, and sometimes the Puffin has to drop part of its catch (usually a dozen or more sandeels) to distract the attacker long enough to make it to the burrow. Pufflings fledge when full-grown and able to fly, and from that point they make their way in the world without the care of a parent. In winter, Puffins' white faces become greyish, making their clownish eyes less obvious, and they also shed the colourful extra plates of keratin that adorn their bills in the breeding season. Puffins are less widespread than Guillemots and Razorbills, with the bulk of their British population confined to just a few Scottish islands.

Kittiwake *Rissa tridactyla*

At first glance this medium-sized, rather dainty gull looks not so different to our other gull species, but it has a much more strictly marine lifestyle and this shows in the way of various small adaptations. For example, it has short, stout legs with no hind toes but very strong claws on the front-pointing toes, better for clinging to rock than running about on flat surfaces. And unlike most other gull chicks,

which are brown-plumaged for camouflage, young Kittiwakes are black, grey and white, with a zigzag pattern across their wings that blends in with the waves on the sea when seen from above. Kittiwakes can be seen gathering clumps of seaweed in spring, which they use to build their nests on cliff ledges – the nests are more compact than typical gull nests, with a deeper cup. They breed around most of our coasts where suitable cliffs (or, in a few cases, tall seaside buildings) are available, and unlike the auks they have a few colonies in south-east England. They feed mainly on fish and are less inclined to scavenge or

exploit unconventional food sources than other gulls.

Fulmar *Fulmarus glacialis*

The order of seabirds known formally as Procellariformes and informally as the 'tubenoses' contains a great diversity of species, ranging from tiny storm-petrels to mighty albatrosses. They have unusually acute senses of smell for birds, and use this ability to locate floating carrion from a long distance. They also catch some living prey, but are built to fly rather than dive. They can cover huge distances over the sea, using the differentials between air currents over and in between

Left With their large dark eyes, Kittiwakes have a gentler look about them than some other gull species.

Above **Above** Fulmars are clumsy on land, but can take off by allowing the wind to catch under their large, long wings.

the wave crests to give them 'free' lift, a flight technique called dynamic soaring, and mainly feed by picking morsels from the surface. The Fulmar is one of four tubenoses that nest on our coast and is much easier to see than the other three, which only come to land at night. With its white body and grey wings, the Fulmar looks rather gull-like, but has a quite different face with its tubular nostrils and frowning dark eye. It also flies quite differently, alternating a stiff-winged glide with a burst of fast flapping, quite unlike the leisurely, 'loose-wristed' flight of

gulls. Very widespread in Britain, Fulmars nest on all kinds of cliffs and (where mammalian predators are absent) clifftops, and occasionally on coastal buildings. They like a wide ledge or gentle slope, often with some vegetation nearby, and pairs tend to be quite well-spaced. Any predator approaching the nest will be repelled by a highly effective defensive strategy – the parent (or the chick, if it is well grown) vomits the stinking, oily contents of its crop at its would-be assailant. If the vomit is really on target, its effect can be devastating – gulls and skuas

sometimes die after being 'Fulmared' as the oil renders them unable to fly well or stay waterproof when swimming. Fulmars rear one chick a year, but make up for their low productivity by being very long-lived – some individuals reach their forties or fifties.

Gannet *Morus bassanus*
A very large, stately and impressive seabird, the Gannet nests on the grassy tops of mammal-free cliffs, islands and sea stacks, in large colonies with the nests close together but very evenly spaced. In flight this bird

Cliffs & headlands

looks cigar-shaped with its tapering head and tail, and is white apart from black wingtips and a lovely ochre flush across the crown and nape. Gannets manage to straddle the two distinct seabird 'professions' of aerial mastery and deep-diving prowess, by means of their spectacular plunge-diving whereby they drop from several metres up and hit the water head-on at a steep angle with wings folded back. Their bodies possess various adaptations to cope with this high-impact feeding style, including having a layer of air-pockets under the skin of their necks which effectively works as biological bubblewrap, cushioning the blow when they hit the water. Even so, Gannets can die in diving accidents – when many birds are diving into the same patch of sea, they may even suffer fatal collisions with each other. The single chick is a naked, lizard-like thing on hatching, but quickly grows a coat of thick white fluff. This is gradually shed as the chick grows, to eventually reveal the chocolate-brown juvenile plumage. It takes several years for this to be replaced with adult white plumage, and so you will see many youngish Gannets with mottled brown and white feathers. These younger birds will not be breeding, but visit colonies to assess the lie of the land and check out possible future nest sites and mates, before making their first breeding attempt at about five or six years old. Gannets have only a few large colonies around Britain, but when not breeding can usually be seen offshore from any coastline.

Shag *Phalacrocorax aristotelis*
You will find odd pairs of Shags among clusters of other seabirds, and often also on more sloping shelves of rock near the sea. These are large, snaky-necked birds which build large

Above Gannets in colonies may argue with their neighbours, but form lasting and affectionate bonds with partners.

Left From bill-tip to tail-tip, the Gannet is perfectly streamlined – essential to allow it to safely plunge-dive deeply for fish.

nests, and need a reasonably broad ledge. From a distance, a Shag just looks plain black, but if you see one close up (as you can at places like the Farne Islands) you'll notice the beautiful green lustre of its plumage, and the way the darker fringes to the glossy green-black back and wing feathers create a beautifully ornate pattern. Shags remain close to their cliffs all year, unlike the other cliff-nesters, and can be seen on the sea diving for fish, or standing on the rocks with wings outstretched, drying off their plumage. This is a necessity due to their lack of effective waterproofing, an unusual trait in a swimming bird but one that allows them to make very energy-efficient dives as they reach neutral buoyancy at much shallower depths than other seabirds. The closely related Cormorant also nests on cliffs, but also in trees and on lake islands inland.

Gulls *Larus species*

Three common species of large gulls will nest on cliffs, although none are strictly cliff specialists. The Herring Gull is the familiar silver-backed gull of seaside towns. The Lesser Black-backed Gull looks similar, but is a little smaller and longer-winged, and its back is dark slaty grey. The Great Black-backed Gull dwarfs the other two – it is a powerhouse of a gull with a massive bill, and has a jet-black back and wings. All three gulls are declining dramatically in the

and Eiders on low ground close to sheltered sea shores. However, sea cliffs are regularly used as breeding sites by a few birds that have no need to go out to sea – these include Peregrine Falcons, Kestrels, Rock Doves (the wild ancestors of our street pigeons), Rock Pipits, Jackdaws, Ravens, Choughs and even White-tailed Eagles.

A WALK ON THE CHALK
Summertime clifftop walks are always interesting for the wildlife-watcher. Even in areas where the cliff-faces themselves

'wilder' parts of their coastal breeding range, but fare better where they breed in towns, perhaps because food is more easily available there. The gulls are not on friendly terms with other seabirds and often attempt to steal the fish they catch, or even predate their nests.

Our other breeding seabirds are not particularly associated with cliffs. Black Guillemots tend to nest on low rocky coasts, boulder beaches, and man-made structures that project into the sea. Storm-petrels and Manx Shearwaters use burrows or natural crevices, almost invariably on islands where there are no rats. Skuas, terns and the smaller gulls tend to nest on lower, level ground, such as beaches or islands within lagoons, or moorland in the case of the skuas. Divers, grebes and most seaducks nest well inland,

Far left Shags need more space than most cliff-nesters, as they build a bulky nest to accommodate two to four chicks.

Top left The Herring Gull is a generalist diet-wise, and will be quick to grab any unattended auk chick on the cliffs.

Left Kestrels are common cliff-nesters, though they move inland rather than out to sea to find food.

Right

Probably the most widespread cliff-nesting seabird, the Fulmar is the only one to breed in good numbers along south-eastern English coasts.

don't hold large seabird colonies, you can still see birds such as Ravens and Peregrine Falcons flying along the cliff edge, and there will probably also be Fulmars and Cormorants around. If the tide is low there may a little exposed flat shore, with waders foraging there, and your high vantage point is good for looking for seabirds on and over the open sea.

With some clifftop walks, though, especially if you are walking atop a stretch of chalk cliff in south-east England, there is as much if not more wildlife interest right by your feet than there is over the sea. Chalk grassland is an important

habitat, and many of the various chalk-loving plants that you'll find here are important for particular insect species.

Two species of blue butterfly both need Horseshoe Vetch plants on which to lay their eggs. The vetch is an attractive plant, producing a circle of bright yellow flowers in spring. It grows only on chalky ground. The Chalkhill Blue is the commoner of the two, and is on the wing in July and August. The rarer Adonis Blue produces two generations of adults each year, the first flying in May to June and the second in August to September. These two butterflies are closely related, and the

females are similar-looking, but the males are easily told apart. Chalkhill males are pale silvery blue on their uppersides, with broad dusky greyish edges to the wings. Adonis males are a deeper, pure and brilliant blue with no dusky edges but a narrow black-and-white chequered margin to each wing. Although the caterpillars of both feed on Horseshoe Vetch, they also need the presence of ants, which tend and guard the caterpillars, in exchange for the sweet secretions the caterpillars produce. The ants, and therefore the caterpillars, only appear to thrive in warm, sheltered situations, where the grass

swared is short enough to allow the sun's warmth to heat up the ground.

Other butterflies to look out for on high chalky grassland include the Small Blue, which is blackish and tiny, the Marbled White with its bold chessboard pattern, and the Dark Green Fritillary, a large butterfly with bright fiery orange wings, marked with intricate black patterning (the 'dark green' of its name refers to the colour of its hindwing undersides). In high summer you will also see masses of black-and-red Six-spot Burnet moths, feeding on nectar-rich flowers such as Wild Thyme and knapweeds.

Above Flowery chalk cliff-tops are home to the lovely Chalkhill Blue butterfly, which is on the wing in July and August.

Left Six-spot Burnet moths fly by day and have a liking for chalky and limestone grassland.

A cliff-top walk offers great scenery, as much fresh air as you can cope with, and great wildlife-watching opportunities.

Clifftops can be very breezy, so seek out sheltered hollows for the best chance of finding interesting insects.

TWITCHING ON THE HEADLANDS

Where a promontory of high rock juts out into the sea much further than the surrounding land, especially on the east coast, there you will find birdwatchers eagerly checking through the scrub and grassland on autumn mornings, in search of rare birds. It is easy to imagine how, as a tired young bird on its first migration flies through bad weather over interminable sea, its spirits may lift as a wedge of land appears out of the mist. It is often strong winds that push migrants to our shores, and bad weather with poor visibility at sea that makes them desperate to find land, where they can rest and feed, and wait for better weather. When the wind and weather conditions come together in just the right way, headlands can play host to huge numbers of migratory birds, which disperse into scrubby patches and sheltered valleys as soon as they arrive, so it can seem that every bush is filled with birds. These 'falls' are rare, but memorable, events.

Usually when there is a big arrival of migrants, the vast majority will be relatively common species. They may include Fieldfares, Redwings, Redstarts, Pied Flycatchers, Chiffchaffs, and even species like Blackbirds, Robins and Goldcrests, which we know as resident birds but which are migratory in the northern European parts of their range. Among them all may be something scarcer – perhaps a Barred Warbler, a Wryneck or a Red-backed Shrike. What

Below The Barred Warbler is one of several migratory eastern European birds that turn up along the east coast of Britain in autumn.

Cliffs & headlands

everyone really hopes to find is a 'mega' – an extreme rarity, with few if any previous British records. Past examples of British 'firsts' found on coastal cliff headlands include an Alder Flycatcher from North America at Land's End, and at the opposite corner of the British Isles, a Brown Shrike from Asia at Sumburgh Head, Shetland. A find as rare as these is big news in the birding world, and can draw quite a crowd if the bird is considerate enough to linger for at least a day or two.

Not all headlands are on high ground. Some sizeable headlands, such as the Dungeness peninsula in Kent and Spurn Head in East Yorkshire, are low-lying and are formed by longshore drift. They, too, can act as magnets for migrating birds, and so do islands and island groups that are positioned such that they are the first landfall after an expanse of open sea. Some of the most productive birding headlands and islands around the coast have their own bird observatories, where migrating birds are trapped to be ringed. There are often vacancies for volunteer helpers at observatories, in various capacities, and spending a week or two at an observatory is a great way for a birder to see many species, perhaps including some rarities, at point-blank range, as well as to learn about the science of migration study.

The other great appeal of

headlands to birders is their value as seawatching spots. Seabirds often migrate past our shores so far out that they will never be seen, even with powerful optics, but they are more likely to pass close to headlands, especially in bad weather. The dedicated seawatcher is a hardy soul, and needs to be, as the best seawatching conditions are on wild autumn mornings when strong onshore winds are blowing and there is also a bit of rain in the air. At a few particularly popular seawatching sites, there are hides or other shelter which makes things a bit more comfortable.

PLACES TO VISIT
Here is a selection of the best cliffs and headlands to see wildlife around the British Isles.

ENGLAND

Durlston Head, Dorset
The Isle of Purbeck, though not actually an island, is a distinct and very beautiful part of Dorset with many wonderful wildlife-watching spots, including RSPB

Left At many headlands, ringing groups trap and ring large numbers of migrating birds (such as this Blackcap) through autumn.

Below The stunning Red-backed Shrike used to breed commonly in Britain, but now is much more likely to be found as a passage migrant on the east coast.

Arne with its heathland birds and views across Poole Harbour, and Studland Beach where all six native British reptiles occur. Durlston Head, at the south-eastern tip of the 'isle', is a high limestone headland topped with chalky grassland, and on the cliff-face you will find one of the very few south-coast seabird colonies that has Guillemots, Razorbills and Shags, as well as the more widespread Kittiwakes and Fulmars. Along the clifftop, downland flowers bloom in profusion and a wonderful array of butterflies is on the wing through the warmer months, with Adonis and Chalkhill Blues, Wall Brown, Marbled White, and the very localised Lulworth Skipper among the highlights.

Portland Bill, Dorset
Another Dorset 'isle', Portland is connected to the mainland by a narrow waist of land, and in contrast to the sandy shores of Weymouth to the east and the famous shingle bar of Chesil Beach to the west, is a high, hulking, 6km by 2.5km chunk of limestone that reaches far out into the English Channel. The southernmost tip is the 'Bill' and is well known as a hotspot for watching seabirds, and for rare migrating songbirds. A very active bird observatory keeps track of daily sightings of all kinds of wildlife. The grassy tops are good for butterflies and flowers, with local specialities including the Portland Sea Lavender, which occurs nowhere

Cliffs & headlands

Far left
Durlston Head in
Dorset has
spectacular
cliff-top walks.

Left Ravens are
thriving on steep
coastlines along
the south coast
of England.

else. Some seabirds nest on the cliffs, and it is a wonderful place to watch Peregrines and Ravens playing in the wind at the edge. There is also a fair chance of spotting cetaceans offshore.

Seaford Head, East Sussex
The walk over Seaford Head from Seaford town to the beautiful Cuckmere valley involves some lung-busting climbs, but is worthwhile for the amazing views. A short way up the first slope, you can see a large chalk stack which is home to one of the very few Kittiwake colonies in the south-east, and the cliffs also have nesting Fulmars, Peregrines and Ravens. Many migrant songbirds use the Head as a launching point for their southwards journey to France and beyond. In spring it is equally good for arriving migrants, with the short turf sometimes festooned with freshly arrived Wheatears in late March.

Spurn Head, East Yorkshire
The long sandy spit at Spurn, reaching across the Humber estuary, is an interesting geological phenomenon. It is formed by longshore drift and is still growing at its tip, but periodically large amounts of material are wiped out by big storm surges, after which it reforms in a slightly different position. The entire spit is gradually shifting westwards, about two metres a year. It stretches nearly 5km into the North Sea, which makes it subject to receiving large 'falls'

of migrating birds when the weather is right. Early mornings after a night of strong easterly winds, between September and November, are the best times to search. There are also estuarine mudflats viewable from the spit, which attract waders.

Above Seaford
Head is home
to south-east
England's
only breeding
Kittiwakes.

Flamborough Head and Bempton Cliffs, North Yorkshire

Flamborough Head is a large headland formed of hard chalk. It is designated an SAC and managed as a nature reserve. Bempton Cliffs are on the northern side of the headland, and are managed by the RSPB. The seabird colony here is the most important mainland colony in England, and has all the expected birds, including Puffins and England's only mainland Gannet colony. The clifftop walks include several observation points from which you can view the seabirds. Flamborough Head has attracted numerous rare migrant birds over the years and is a popular autumn destination for rarity hunters.

St Bees Head, Cumbria

This headland is home to the largest seabird colony on the west side of England. It is managed by the RSPB, and there is a clifftop path running about 4kn which takes you past three viewing platforms. As well as the usual seabird suspects on the cliffs, there are also a few pairs of Black Guillemots here, and they can be see all year round as they do not head for the open sea in winter like the other auk species.

WALES

Strumble Head, Pembrokeshire

This is one of the best seawatching sites in Wales, and indeed Britain, and keen seawatchers here regularly find scarce species like Cory's Shearwater and Pomarine Skua among large numbers of the more common species. An old Second World War searchlight station has been converted into a makeshift hide, so you can enjoy the birds in comfort even when it is blowing a gale outside. On fine days a clifftop walk is most enjoyable and there is a good chance of seeing Chough and Peregrine, and seals offshore

South Stack, Anglesey

This is an important seabird colony, topped with maritime heathland which is itself a rich wildlife habitat. One of the special insects of this maritime heath is the Silver-studded Blue butterfly, which emerges in July and can be incredibly abundant. Look out for Adders on the heath as well, along with attractive plant life such as Heath Spotted Orchids and Spotted Rock Rose. As well as the Ravens and Peregrines that haunt most

Right Spurn Head is a remarkable geological phenomenon and a very important headland for recording bird migration.

cliffsides, there are Choughs here, cutting a distinctive outline with their long curved bills and penchant for aerobatics. The cliffs have all four British auks, Black Guillemots being close to their southern limit here.

SCOTLAND

St Abb's Head, Borders

This NNR and National Trust site offers spectacular scenery, the craggy coastline featuring stacks and islets, chiselled cliff edges

Above
Strumble Head in Pembrokeshire is a great vantage point to look for rare seabirds offshore in autumn.

Left Cliff-tops hold their own unique assemblages of flowers.

South Stack cliffs are stunningly scenic and
home to some rare species, including Choughs.

and wave-cut platforms below. The 60,000 or so seabirds that nest here are a mixture of Guillemots, Razorbills, Shags, Puffins, Kittiwakes and Harring Gulls. The flowery clifftops are home to the Northern Brown Argus butterfly, a dainty member of the blue family, and as a bonus the artificial Mire Loch, just inland, attracts many freshwater birds, as well as some of the seabirds which come to bathe.

Troup Head, Aberdeenshire
An RSPB reserve on the quiet coast south of the Moray Firth, Troup Head has precipitous cliffs with huge numbers of seabirds,

Right Black Guillemots breed at South Stack, look out for them on low rocks near the sea.

Below The coastline at St Abb's Head is dramatic and varied.

including a sizeable mainland gannetry. Follow the path down through flowery fields to reach vantage points over the cliffs, and enjoy watching Fulmars, auks, Kittiwakes and Gannets flying past at eye-level. The colony is sometimes 'buzzed' by visiting Great Skuas, and butterflies visiting the meadows include the Dark Green Fritillary.

Fowlsheugh, Aberdeenshire
The cliffs at this SSSI and RSPB reserve stand 70 metres high, and through spring and summer resonate to the deafening voices of some 130,000 nesting seabirds. You can see them from the clifftop path, along which you'll find a shiny new RSPB viewing shelter, or for a different perspective take a boat trip along the coast from Stonehaven. Butterflies on the flowery clifftops include Grayling, Scotch Argus and Northern Brown Argus, and a look out to sea may produce sightings of seals, dolphins and even Minke Whales.

Sumburgh Head, Shetland
The archipelagos of Orkney and Shetland, as well as the Western Isles on the other side of Scotland, hold the biggest concentrations of nesting seabirds in the whole of the British Isles. While many important seabird colonies are on tiny uninhabited islands, Sumburgh Head is on Mainland, Shetland, and easily reached by road from the main town of Lerwick. It holds a large seabird colony, and is also a superb spot to look for marine mammals, including Orcas, from the high clifftops.

IRELAND

Bridges of Ross, Co Clare
Only one 'bridge' is left at this wild cliff coast in south-west Ireland, the other sea arches having collapsed, which may

Below A Great Black-backed Gull flies along the cliff-edge at Troup Head, looking out for the chance to steal an egg or chick from another seabird.

Below With great good luck you could see an Orca from the cliffs of Sumburgh Head, Shetland.

Far right The Cliffs of Moher, in County Clare, have nesting seabirds and unusual invertebrates.

deter you from walking across the bridge that remains, but there are many other spots to walk or just sit. In autumn, birdwatchers come in droves to do the latter, training their telescopes on the expanse of the Atlantic in the hope that rare seabirds will fly past. Extreme rarities that have been seen here include Fea's Petrel, a globally threatened species that breeds only on the Cape Verde Islands and Madeira Islands, while scarce species such as Long-tailed Skua sometimes go by in impressive numbers. The various other headlands prominent headlands in Co. Clare and also Co. Kerry and Co. Cork can also offer spectacular seawatching.

Cliffs of Moher, Co Clare

The 120-metre cliffs at the south-western edge of the flat, rocky moonscape of the Burren are home to tens of thousands of nesting seabirds, including Puffins. You may also see Choughs and Ravens, and the cliffs command wonderful views along the coast. It is also well worth visiting the Burren itself – 250 square kilometres of 'karst landscape', which holds a huge variety of plantlife and is also excellent for insects. Local specialities include the Burren Green moth, and the beetle *Ochthebius nilsonni*, which is only found at four other sites in the world.

Cliffs & headlands

Urban coasts

People like to live by the sea for all sorts of reasons. Today, the motivation is often more esoteric than it may have been many years ago, when sea fishing and sea trade were more important industries than they are now. Irrespective of the 'whys', the 'hows' remain broadly the same. People need a certain level of infrastructure, they need housing, transport and other facilities, and constructing these means removing – or at least dramatically changing – sizeable areas of wildlife habitat. Nevertheless, seaside towns have their own special wildlife communities, composed of species which have learned to live alongside humanity, and (for some people at least) their presence adds greatly to the charm and enjoyment of living on the seaside. Some coastal towns are actually interesting wildlife-watching destinations in their own right, with things to see that aren't found in the wider coastal countryside.

ANATOMY OF A SEASIDE TOWN

Most seaside settlements were originally based around fishing or trading, while others were founded with the intention that they would serve as resorts – coastal retreats for the well-to-do, who wished to 'take the sea air'. You can find examples of all in close proximity to each other: on the south-east coast there is the major port of Dover, then heading west you reach Hastings, a fishing town which still has the largest beach-based fishing fleet in England, and the next sizeable town along is Eastbourne, planned and built in the mid-19th century as a resort 'by gentlemen for gentlemen'.

Right These Turnstones and dozens of their fellows live happily amidst the bustle at Newlyn harbour in west Cornwall

Below Hastings in East Sussex offers a rare example of a beach-launched fishing fleet.

Today, though, tourism is the most important industry for the majority of seaside towns, which has led to considerable convergence in their general character. The seasonal nature of most tourism work means that some seaside towns, especially those that are not in easy reach of a major city, may be affected by poverty and social deprivation. Others are prosperous, with high-end galleries and restaurants that bring in business even out of season, and these attractions keep visitors returning year after year. Wildlife tourism is a growing industry that is increasingly exploited in seaside towns that lie close to seabird cliffs or good feeding areas for cetaceans, and some wildlife tourism takes place in the low season. Seaside towns typically have a beach and a beachfront road and path or promenade, with various attractions on the beach side. Many have a pier and some formal gardens, and tall buildings on the beachfront. For some birds, beachfront buildings are a perfectly acceptable alternative to a steep cliff-face.

ROOFTOP GULLS

Buildings may not be sufficiently cliff-like to convince Guillemots and Razorbills to nest on them, but gulls, the great opportunists of the seabird world, have no such qualms. They usually opt to nest on flat parts of rooftops, or tucked between chimney pots at

Above Some seaside towns, like Eastbourne in East Sussex, began life as tourist resorts for the well-to-do.

Left Sporting and leisure activities like kayaking provide revenue for seaside towns.

the tops of sloped, gable-style roofs. In some towns, a view out over the rooftops in summer will reveal pretty much one gull nest on every building. All those gulls need food supplies – in towns that have a fishing industry, much of that food will come from scraps thrown from boats, and fish that the gulls catch for themselves. Elsewhere, though, the gulls will make their living by scavenging on the streets, visiting refuse tips and (to the dismay of the town's human residents) raiding the bins. For a bird as versatile and enterprising as a gull, food can always be found. It is good, safe nest sites that are at a premium.

The most common rooftop gull around Britain is the Herring Gull. With its snowy-white head and body plumage, silver back and wings, and neatly white-spotted black wingtips, it is an elegant and striking bird, though with a certain toughness of expression thanks to its yellow eyes and disapprovingly downturned mouthline. It is also a large bird, nearly four times as heavy as a pigeon (which for people who aren't keen on birds is already quite large enough), with long strong wings and an intimidating pickaxe bill. Add to this its loud and unmelodic voice, the mess it can make and its tendency to become a little over-defensive when rearing chicks, and it is understandable that not all people who live by the sea are gull fans.

But in many ways, seaside towns provide a perfect environment for gulls to live and breed, and it should be no surprise that they are surviving better in the urban environment than on wilder coastlines. Looking at the British Isles as a whole, there are still far more Herring Gulls living rurally than in towns, but the rural populations are in major trouble. Since 1969–1970, the Herring Gull population in the UK has more than halved, and the situation is similar in Ireland. This decline means the bird is red-listed as a species of conservation concern. Because they are doing a little better than rural colonies, urban colonies are making up an increasingly large proportion of the total population – in the UK from less than one per cent in the 1970s to 14 per cent by the start of the 21st century.

If wheelie-bins or other secure ways to dispose of household waste are provided, this will eliminate the problems of gulls ripping up binbags and throwing the contents around the street. Gulls can be discouraged from nesting on rooftops by putting guards up around chimneys or other spots large enough for a nest. A more difficult problem, luckily not a universal one, concerns gulls that have become so bold around humankind that they will effectively 'mug' people for food – visitors to St Ives, in Cornwall, are well advised to take care when enjoying fish and chips on the beach, as the gulls are quite willing and able to intercept food that is on its way from hand to

Below Chimney pots offer good launchpads and vantage spots for Herring Gulls, and the spaces between the stacks are often perfect for nesting.

urban coasts

Left Young Herring Gulls beg for food by tapping at the red spot on their parent's bill, while making a plaintive whistling call.

mouth. Discouraging people from directly feeding the gulls is a sensible strategy to help reduce the problem, and some local authorities have taken the stop of issuing 'on the spot' fines to people caught doing this. Perhaps the most intractable gull 'issue' is that of divebombing people and pets when the gulls have chicks in the nest, although this habit is certainly not universal.

THE TROUBLED HISTORY OF THE BLACK RAT

In Britain, the near universal dislike of wild rats has many justifications, but none more so than the fact that it was rats – or specifically their fleas – that brought the Black Death to our shores. The bubonic plague is a bacterial infection, carried by

Other rooftop seabirds

The Lesser Black-backed Gull is another rooftop-nester. It is less common in seaside towns than the Herring Gull, but has some significant urban colonies further inland. It, too, is a species of conservation concern, amber-listed in both the UK and Ireland. Its larger relative, the Great Black-backed Gull, is beginning to try out urban living as well, though the number of rooftop pairs at the moment is still very small. It, too, is amber-listed in both the UK and Ireland. The rarest gull that may be found setting up home on your roof is the Yellow-legged Gull, a southern European species which nests in tiny numbers on the south coast. Some of its pairings are mixed-species, the Yellow-legged being quite happy to pair up with a Herring Gull or Lesser Black-backed Gull if it cannot find another Yellow-legged.

The Kittiwake, most maritime of our gulls, is a cliff-face nester, but there is a famous colony on the towers that support the Tyne Bridge and on other nearby buildings in Newcastle. While this colony has many supporters, it has caused some local discord with not everyone appreciating the birds' constant calling through the breeding season. In a few areas, Fulmars have also taken to nesting on seafront buildings.

Right The appealing-looking Black Rat was the carrier of fleas that spread the bubonic plague in the 14th century. They are now very rare in the UK.

Below Lundy Island, one of the last refuges of the Black Rat until an eradication programme removed them from the Island

fleas and passed to humans from flea bites. Without treatment it will kill two out of three infected people, and when it struck England in the 14th century, it killed more than half of the total population of three million, and across Europe accounted for an estimated 25 million lives. This massive crash in the human population led to some radical reformations in social structure, some of them very positive, but it was an extremely heavy price to pay for progress.

The rat responsible was not the familiar and common Brown Rat that lives throughout Britain today, but its smaller, more elegant and darker relative, the Black Rat (sometimes known as

the Ship Rat). Both rat species are native to Asia and are introduced aliens to our shores, the Black Rat arriving in Roman times and the Brown Rat much more recently, in the early 18th century. Being adaptable, adventurous and adept at chewing, rats have been stowing away on ships since there first were ships, accessing the crew's food stores with ease to sustain them through the voyage, and disembarking at the destination to continue doing what they do best – surviving, and reproducing. Worldwide, ship-hitching Brown, Black and Pacific Rats have colonised places thousands of kilometres away from their native lands, and between them have wiped out a dizzying number of native

species, especially on small islands which knew no natural predators before the rats showed up.

The Black Rat was formerly common throughout Britain, but since the Brown Rat arrived it has declined enormously, its distribution shrinking back to the major sea ports where it first became established. Here, too, its numbers have dwindled as rodent control measures have improved. Today, the total population in Britain is only about 1,300, nearly all restricted to a few coastal towns. In 2014, funding and permission was given to eradicate a population on the Shiant Islands in western Scotland, as the rats pose a threat to seabirds by preying on their eggs and small chicks. An eradication project on Lundy has already been completed.

For many mammal-watchers in Britain today, the Black Rat is regarded as an interesting species worth seeking out, rather than a dangerous pest. Its longer history in Britain than the Brown Rat, its more appealing appearance than its burly cousin, its decline at the paws of that cousin, and its great scarcity today all contribute to a somewhat positive impression. There is an argument that, as a resident of our lands for more than 2,000 years, and an integral part of our history, it should now be protected, and not allowed to decline further. However, it is still a non-native and invasive species, which without the Brown Rat around would undoubtedly be just as hugely abundant, problematic and unpopular as the Brown Rat is now.

PORTRAIT OF A HARBOUR

For centuries, humans have been doing what longshore drift does naturally, and building barriers across bays to create inlets which are sheltered from the open sea. Harbours provide safe, still places for boats to be moored, and infrastructure is added to make it easy to load and unload, refuel and carry out maintenance. A large working

Below

Mevagissey in Cornwall is a particularly picturesque harbour, busy with fishing boats and pleasure craft.

Top In stormy weather, harbours offer a refuge for seabirds, including rarities like this Kumlien's Gull.

Centre The piles of nets, rope and lobster pots in fishing harbours are foraging grounds for Rock Pipits.

Right The combination of mild coastal weather and early-flowering garden plants make south coast seaside towns good places to spot emerging spring butterflies like Small Tortoiseshells.

harbour is a colourful and busy place, and it can also be a good place to observe wildlife, especially if used by fishing boats. Fish discards thrown into the harbour water will invariably attract gulls, while on the concrete parts of the harbour there will be other foraging birdlife.

A visit to the harbour of a fishing port in winter can be extremely rewarding for the wildlife-watcher. The congregations of gulls may include the odd scarcity, with the so-called 'white-winged gulls' becoming more and more frequent the further north and west you head. Ports in Ireland and northern Scotland may attract double figures of Iceland and Glaucous Gulls, two very similar Arctic-breeding gulls which visit the British Isles in winter. Adults of both species look like very pale Herring Gulls but with pure white wingtips, while young birds are the colour

Urban coasts

of weak milky tea and become paler with successive moults. The two species are best distinguished by size – Iceland is smaller than a Herring Gull while Glaucous is considerably bigger. A Canadian subspecies of Iceland Gull also sometimes turns up here – Kumlien's Gull has smoky-grey wingtips with large white spots.

Other birds may come into the harbour to catch fish rather than to scavenge for scraps thrown from the boats. They include Guillemots, Razorbills, Cormorants, Shags and divers, and with luck you can see all of them at very close range. After severe storms at sea, more pelagic seabirds may head into the harbour for shelter – it is always worth visiting the morning after a stormy night, to look for Sabine's Gulls, Gannets, shearwaters, Leach's Storm-petrels and the like. On the concreted parts of the harbour there may be flocks of Turnstones, which check over

piles of nets and lobster pots, and in some areas will mill around people's feet, as tame as pigeons, and eagerly hoover up dropped chips and whatever else they can find. Equally confiding Rock Pipits are also found in many harbours. Harbours that attract many birds may also attract Peregrines, which increasingly are nesting on town buildings as well as the more traditional cliff-faces. The interest is not limited to birds, either. A few large ports still have populations of the rare Black Rat, and at the harbour mouth you may be lucky enough to spot a seal or even a dolphin.

PLACES TO VISIT
Here is a selection of the best seaside towns to look for wildlife around the British Isles.

ENGLAND

Penzance, Cornwall
The huge, picturesque sweep of Mount's Bay, near the very tip of

Cornwall, is somewhat sheltered from the open Atlantic and so draws in many seabirds in the winter months. Penzance is a great base from which to explore, but there is also interesting wildlife to see without leaving the town at all. Look offshore for Great Northern Divers, auks, Shags, seaducks and other seabirds. Purple Sandpipers join Turnstones on the shoreline, and the rocks around the Jubilee Pool provide them with a high-tide roost – you may also see Black Redstarts here. Often, solitary Grey Seals make their way by a short distance offshore. The position of the town means that spring arrives early here – in March look out for the first Sandwich Terns, Swallows and Sand Martins, and on warm days for the first Small Tortoiseshell and Peacock butterflies coming out of hibernation.

Weymouth, Dorset
Weymouth is a special town for

Above

Radipole Lake is a wonderful wetland nature reserve in the heart of the Dorset seaside town of Weymouth.

It may not be the most picturesque stretch of coast, but the Hartlepool area has long been something of a mecca for birdwatchers.

wildlife-watchers, because it contains two excellent RSPB reserves, one of them right in the heart of town. Radipole Lake is a collection of lagoons, surrounded by reedbeds, near the mouth of the River Wey, which runs through the reserve. Enter the reserve alongside the incongruous surroundings of a retail park, and within minutes you can be listening to Cetti's Warblers and watching Marsh Harriers. The other reserve, Lodmoor, lies on the north-eastern edge of the town. Like Radipole Lake it has open water and reedbeds, and also patches of grassland. Weymouth is also ideally placed to explore Portland and Chesil Beach.

Southend, Essex

This town, along with neighbouring Westcliff-on-Sea and Shoeburyness, lies on the northern side of the Thames estuary. Best known as a cheap-and-cheerful resort town with all the trappings that includes, Southend is also a great place to see interesting winter birdlife in the sheltered mouth of the Thames. From the very long pier, you can see Red-throated Divers, Kittiwakes, Mediterranean Gulls, auks and other seabirds, often both Grey and Common Seals. There are some excellent nature reserves locally, including Two-tree island which plays host to roosting waders when the estuary mud is covered at high tide, and further west on the tidal Vange Creek is Wat Tyler Country Park, which has scrub and reedbeds and attracts many birds – it is also a regular site for some rare insects including the Scarce Migrant Hawker dragonfly.

Hartlepool, Co Durham

With a rocky east-facing headland, a sheltered harbour and a sweeping bay leading round to the mudflats and

Below The thriving Red Kite is among the wildlife treats to be seen near Cardigan Bay.

Urban coasts

Left The pools and reedbeds at the Montrose basin nature reserve are great for wildlife all year round.

saltmarsh of the Tees estuary, Hartlepool holds a wealth of excellent wildlife habitats. The headland is a hot-spot for migrant birds in autumn when easterly winds are blowing, and is a great spot for seawatching. The estuary is vital for shorebirds and wildfowl through autumn and winter into early spring. Hartlepool has an impressive six Local Nature Reserves, including Hart Warren Dunes which holds Burnt-tip Orchids and Northern Brown Argus butterflies.

WALES

New Quay, Ceredigion
This small town on the north-facing coast of Cardigan Bay in west Wales is well known as a great place to look for marine wildlife. In particular, a pod of Bottlenose Dolphins that live in Cardigan Bay are regularly seen from the town's sandy beaches, and even Leatherback Turtles are occasionally seen. Also sometimes seen are Harbour Porpoises and Basking Sharks. The rocky parts of the beaches are excellent for rockpooling, and local birdlife includes Choughs and Red Kites.

SCOTLAND

Montrose, Angus
On the northern, outer edge of the Montrose basin, Montrose town is an ideal place to explore this exceptional enclosed estuary. In summer there is a busy colony of Arctic and Common Terns here and also nesting Sand Martins, while in winter the estuary is taken over by huge flocks of Pink-footed Geese – up to 60,000 at peak times in early winter – and other wildfowl, with waders visiting the shoreline. Seals haul out on the banks, and you could also see Harbour Porpoises. The Scottish Wildlife Trust's visitor centre here, a short distance from the town, has nature trails, four birdwatching hides, and a busy programme of family events.

Banff/Macduff, Aberdeenshire
These two small towns lie either side of the mouth of the river Deveron, which opens out into the sheltered Banff Bay. Each town has a small harbour, and the harbour walls are great vantage points across the bay and the open sea. Here in summer you'll see numerous seabirds commuting to and fro, many of them from the large seabird colony of Troup Head just

Below The male Long-tailed Duck in winter plumage is a gorgeous bird, and can be seen in good numbers in the Moray Firth.

along the coast. In winter, look out for seaducks including Eider, Long-tailed Duck and scoters. There is also a chance of seeing cetaceans here, including the famous Moray Firth Bottlenose Dolphins.

Oban, Argyll

Oban is the starting point for ferry crossings to Mull and further out to the Western Isles, and so is a much used stop-over place for people on their way to one of these wonderful wildlife-rich destinations. Oban Harbour is well-known as a site to see Black Guillemots – several pairs of these charming small auks nest in holes in the wall by the

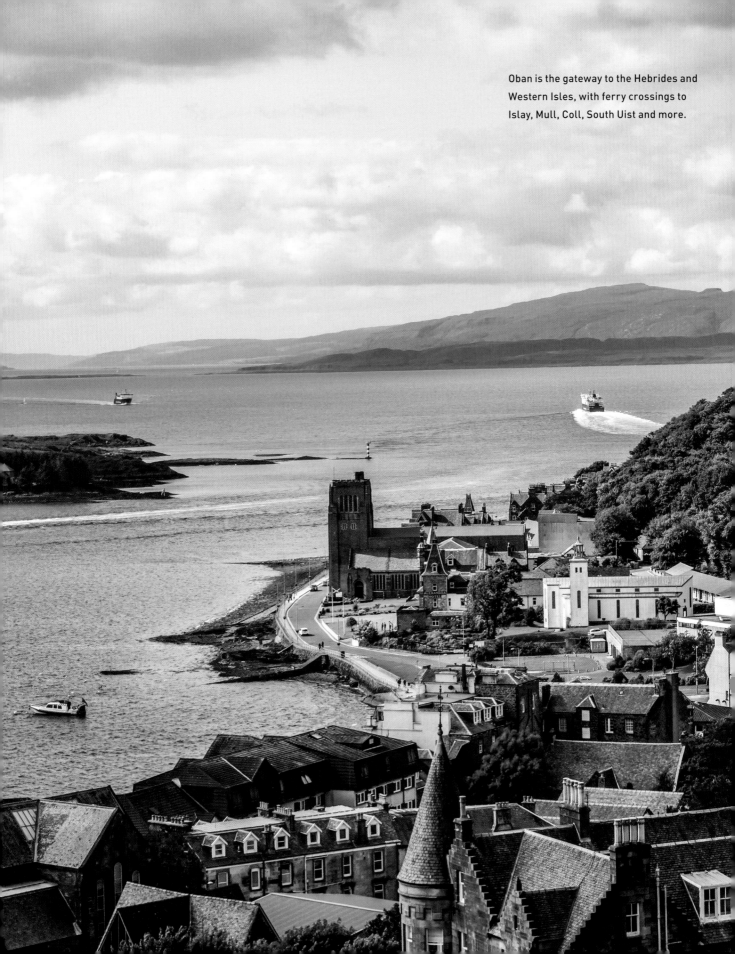

Oban is the gateway to the Hebrides and Western Isles, with ferry crossings to Islay, Mull, Coll, South Uist and more.

Above Look out for Black Guillemots if you're taking a ferry out of Oban harbour.

promenade. You may also see various terns and seals here, and if you go offshore there is the chance of a wider range of other seabirds and also some of the marine mammals.

IRELAND

Dublin, Co Dublin

The sea front at Dublin, and the mouth of the Liffey, offer city birdwatching in an impressive scale. Winter is the best season, when white-winged gulls and Mediterranean Gulls may join the commoner species around the port, and you could also see Guillemot and Brent Goose of the pale-bellied subspecies. Grey Seals may be seen in the river mouth. Bull Island, a 5km vegetated sandbank reachable by a road bridge from the city, is an NNR and has nesting Little Terns, as well as some interesting plantlife including various orchid species. It is also a favoured spot for seals to rest.

Galway, Co Galway

Nimmo's Pier in Galway City is well-known as a site for winter gull-watching. Iceland, Glaucous and Mediterranean Gulls are all regular, and the Ring-billed Gull from North America is also a frequent visitor. Look for Brent Geese and wader flocks on the beach, and there is also the chance of seeing an Otter. Lough Atalia in Galway Bay attracts waders and wildfowl, the latter including a flock of some 50 Scaup, along

with Red-breasted Merganser and Goldeneye.

Killybegs, Co Donegal

The large fishing port is another excellent site for white-winged gulls; both Iceland and Glaucous Gulls are regularly counted in double-figures. The site has also attracted the very rare Thayer's Gull, a North American species – the first record of the species for Europe was here in 1998, and there have since been at least two others at the harbour. Other birds that you may see in the harbour include Black Guillemot and Great Northern Diver.

Left Little Terns nest on Bull Island, near Dublin.

Below Killybegs is probably the most important fishing port in Ireland.

Islands & open sea

The British Isles is an archipelago of more than 6,000 islands, the vast majority of which are tiny and uninhabited. Small islands naturally host fewer species than large ones, and the more remote an island is from the mainland, the fewer species it tends to have. However, islands that have no resident human population can be absolute wildlife havens, in terms of numbers if not necessarily variety. There is also much to see when you leave the mainland behind and strike out over the open sea, whether you are taking a boat out to an island, or just going for a wildlife-watching 'pelagic' boat trip.

Above The Bass Rock is almost entirely covered by nesting Gannets.

THE ISLAND EFFECT

Small islands, isolated from the mainland for thousands of years, tend to have relatively few land animals. Even if terrestrial species were present at a point in the island's history where sea levels were lower and it was connected to a larger land mass, when the sea rose and the island became cut off, any land animals living on it at that time would be at a distinct disadvantage. They would have a small population, and so a high risk of inbreeding and also a high risk that the whole population would fall victim to some local catastrophe. If the island was formerly sea-covered and became exposed as a result of a fall in sea level, it could only be colonised by species that could reach it from the mainland, which excluded most land animals (and also plants – only those with wind-borne, sea-borne or bird-carried seeds would become established).

There are a few land animals that survive on small islands – some inhabited them before the island was cut off from the mainland, but a few must have reached the island by crossing water. They may have been introduced by humans, or perhaps made it to the shore by a fluke ('rafting' – catching a ride on floating debris – is one way that land animals are thought to have colonised some islands). Isolated from others of their kind, they can only reproduce with each other, and tend to evolve in a slightly different direction to mainland populations, with natural selection favouring the particular set of traits that are best suited to life on that one individual island. The same thing may happen with some smaller birds, which would not normally undertake sea crossings of any distance. For example, the Wrens that live on Fair Isle have evolved to be a distinct subspecies to mainland Wrens – the same has happened with the Wrens on St Kilda.

Larger, strongly flying birds, on the other hand, have no problems reaching offshore islands. And for seabirds, islands are dream homes as they are

Islands & open sea

usually entirely free of rats, mustelids and other land animals that can make life difficult for the birds when trying to nest. An island extensively populated by nesting seabirds develops its own particular ecology, with a distinct community of plants growing on the land where the birds nest. The range of species found nesting on islands is broadly similar to that of mainland cliffs, but because they have no concerns about mammalian predators the birds will use much lower and more sloping cliffs than they will on the mainland. Seals also appreciate the lack of disturbance on islands, and use island beaches to rest and to have their pups.

THE NIGHT WATCH

Some of the islands off the west coast of Britain hold our most mysterious nesting seabirds. These are the Manx Shearwater, the European Storm-petrel, and Leach's Storm-petrel. All three species are small, delicate, and lightweight seabirds – the European Storm-petrel is barely larger than a House Sparrow. But they are capable of great endurance, flying to the southern hemisphere each year after breeding to exploit the austral summer. They are also, like all 'tubenoses', amazingly long-lived, with the tiny storm-petrels able to live into their thirties and Manx Shearwaters even longer.

These seabirds are at their most vulnerable when they come to land. Expert in the air and competent on the water, they are rather awkward on terra firma and would be easy prey for large gulls and skuas. For this reason, they only come ashore at night, when they stand a better chance of avoiding these predators, and they nest in burrows, crevices and other small holes that are inaccessible to the larger birds. They can only successfully nest in places where there are no rats or other small mammalian predators that could enter their nest holes, and as a result, nearly all populations live on offshore islands.

Visiting a shearwater or petrel island in summer to see the birds returning to their nests is a magical, almost spooky

Below Grey Seals hauled out on a tiny rocky islet off the Northumberland coast.

Observatories & oddities

As we saw in Chapter 6, headlands on the mainland are very good places to watch for migrant birds, as they are the first landfall for birds crossing the seas. Certain islands are positioned just right to receive migrating birds as well, and a few are so notorious for this that keen birdwatchers make annual pilgrimages to them in the autumn, hoping to see some exceptional rarities. Top of the list are Fair Isle in the Shetlands, and the Isles of Scilly off Cornwall, and there is something of a friendly rivalry between the two. Fair Isle's position means it is more likely to receive migrants from eastern Europe and Siberia, while Scilly has a great record for North American birds, but both have recorded extreme rarities from both directions.

On Fair Isle and some other small islands, visitors can stay at the bird observatory, in comfortable if not luxurious accommodation. One of the main advantages of staying on a tiny island at peak migration time is that if a rare bird does touch down, it will very probably be found by one of the birdwatchers present and seen by the rest, even if it quickly moves on. Visitors to the Scillies have a more difficult job, as the rarities could be found on any of the five inhabited islands, and it is possible to rack up a sizeable bill on the inter-island ferries.

Left Manx Shearwaters spend the daylight hours (and the night-time when not breeding) wandering widely offshore.

experience. The shearwaters gather in rafts on the sea nearby as dusk approaches, but the petrels hang back until it is as dark as it is going to get (never all that dark in a Shetland summer) before flying ashore. They have no fear of humans and will flutter past and around you like bats as each individual scrambles to get to its burrow, and their haunting calls are everywhere. The single chick in each nest can fast for a day or more while waiting for its parents to return, and will then receive a generous meal of regurgitated fish and other marine delights. In the case of the Manx Shearwater, the parents feed the chick until it weighs considerably more than they do, and then they abandon it. Several days later, having

slimmed down a little and accepted that mum and dad are not coming back, it leaves its burrow and flies out to sea, to begin its independent life.

SEA MAMMALS

The British Isles are well-placed for superb whale-watching, especially along the west coast. While you may be lucky enough to see whales and dolphins from land (and in fact there are a few areas where seeing dolphins from the shore is quite regular), to dramatically improve your chances you will need to take a boat trip out to deeper water. Whale-watching boat trips are growing in popularity in Britain and the teams on board are expert at both finding and identifying cetaceans. The two species of seals that live around

our coasts are easier to see, though can be a little tricky to tell apart.

Here are some of the species you are most likely to encounter.

Harbour Porpoise *Phocoena phocoena* This small, shy porpoise is fairly common in sheltered water close to the shore around the British Isles, although it is declining. You will rarely see any more of it than the

Above Boats used for wildlife pelagic trips are usually either small cruisers like this, or RIBs (rigid-hulled inflatable boats), which offer a faster but bumpier ride.

hump of its grey back, which is topped with a small, triangular dorsal fin.

Common Dolphin *Delphinus delphis* A very beautiful, long-beaked dolphin with a dark grey back, yellowish sides, and a lighter grey patch behind its dorsal fin, this species is found off northern and western coasts especially, and is the dolphin most likely to approach boats and ride their bow waves, making for some wonderful close views.

Bottlenose Dolphin *Tursiops truncatus* The familiar 'Flipper' dolphin with its trademark

Right A rare clear view of a Harbour Porpoise reveals the blunt head shape.

Below The Common Dolphin is a delight to watch, often closely approaching boats and bow-riding, with frequent spectacular leaps.

Islands & open sea

cheery expression, this is a large, uniformly grey dolphin which may be seen anywhere around Britain, but has resident populations in the Moray Firth and Cardigan Bay. Occasionally, lone male Bottlenoses take up

long-term residence in bays or harbours.

White-beaked Dolphin
Lagenorhynchus albirostris
Found from western Ireland across to the northern North Sea, this dolphin has a dark grey upperside with a broad pale streak along its sides, and a short, blunt, white beak. The Atlantic White-sided Dolphin is similar but has a black beak and a more obviously white side patch.

Orca *Orcinus orca* Although sometimes known as the Killer Whale, this unmistakeable black-

and-white cetacean with its distinctive long and upright dorsal fin is actually a (very) large dolphin. It is most likely to be seen in the far north, with Shetland being a particular hotspot.

Minke Whale *Balaenoptera acutorostrata* This is the smallest and commonest of the 'baleen' whales that you are likely to see from anywhere in the British Isles. It is most often seen off northern and western coasts. It reaches up to about 10 metres long, and shows a small, strongly hooked dorsal fin. This whale can be very active and may be seen

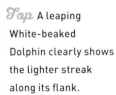

Top A leaping White-beaked Dolphin clearly shows the lighter streak along its flank.

Left A summer boat trip off the west coast is your best bet for meeting a Minke Whale.

breaching (rearing almost fully out of the water).

Fin Whale *Balaenoptera physalus* The second-largest whale (and therefore the second-largest of any kind of animal) in the world, the Fin Whale is mostly seen between north Scotland and south-west Ireland, but also in the Bay of Biscay and up to the south-western tip of England.

Grey Seal *Halichoerus grypus* This is the larger of our seal species, although age and sex differences mean there is a lot of overlap. The Grey Seal occurs around all coastlines and is the species you are most likely to see on its own, swimming or resting in the water very close inshore. It is also more frequent along rocky coasts than the Common Seal. It shows a 'roman-nosed' profile, most obvious in the adult bulls, and almost parallel nostril slits.

Common Seal *Phoca vitulina* This seal has a more dog-like look than the Grey Seal, with a dip between forehead and muzzle. Its nostrils form a V shape, and when you can see the whole animal it looks proportionately very small-headed compared to the Grey Seal, and tends to rest with both head and tail-end raised, giving it a 'banana' shape. It is most likely to be seen in groups, hauled out and resting on sandy beaches or sandbars by sheltered water.

THE UNDERSEA WORLD
Boat trips in search of wildlife tend to concentrate on seabirds and cetaceans, but for a look at the marine world below you, a trip on a glass-bottomed boat can be an enjoyable way to do this without getting wet. You could enjoy close views of marine fish, corals, beautiful varied forests of seaweeds, jellyfish and even seals and seabirds swimming underwater. If getting

wet isn't an issue, there are numerous sites around the British Isles that offer safe snorkelling and scuba-diving.

When arranging a boat trip or a dive, always check that the organisers are committed to looking after the wildlife that you'll be approaching, and keeping disturbance to a minimum. The WiSe scheme is an organisation that trains and gives accreditation to marine wildlife tour operators for responsible conduct towards wildlife – you can find out more about the scheme and see a list of accredited operators by visiting wisescheme.org.

PLACES TO VISIT
Here is a selection of the best small islands for coastal wildlife and the best wildlife-watching boat trips that you can join around the British Isles.

ENGLAND

Isles of Scilly, Cornwall
These beautiful islands lie 45km off the tip of Cornwall and are home to a little over 2,100 people, most of them on St Mary's, the largest island. The entire archipelago is designated an AONB. Although best known as a destination for 'twitchers' in autumn, Scilly has much to offer the keen wildlife-watcher all year round. Seabirds breeding here include small numbers of Manx Shearwaters and European Storm-petrels, and the diverse plantlife includes several

Right
Smaller and more snub-nosed than the Grey Seal, the Common Seal is less widespread than the Grey, and less likely to be seen alone.

Islands & open sea

endemic species including Dwarf Pansy and Orange Birdfoot. Boat trips out from the Scillies offer the chance to see the cetaceans and rare seabirds that are drawn to the rich feeding grounds on the edge of the Bay of Biscay.

Boat trips from Falmouth, Cornwall

Interesting wildlife-watching trips are run from both the north and south coasts of Cornwall, with the lively port town of Falmouth offering several.

Wildlife you could see includes seabirds nesting along the coast, Manx Shearwaters feeding further out, and there is a chance of finding Common Dolphins, Basking Sharks and Sunfish.

Lundy Island, Devon

This beautiful little grass-topped island in the Bristol Channel is managed by the Landmark Trust for the National Trust, and is the only Marine Nature Reserve in England. Visitors can come for the day, or stay in one of the 23

Above Tresco is the second largest of the Scilly Isles, and lies just to the east of Bryher, the smallest inhabited island.

Right Kittiwakes are one of several seabirds that nest on Lundy island.

Above Try an autumn cruise out of Bridlington for the chance to see Arctic Skuas and other less common seabirds.

self-catering cottages. The cliffs hold many nesting Kittiwakes and auks, including a small number of Puffins, and its more obscure residents include an endemic species of weevil! The protected status of the seas around Lundy means that the area is exceptionally rich in marine wildlife, and divers can enjoy seeing rare sponges, corals and sea fans, though for most the highlight is swimming with Grey Seals.

Boat trips from Bridlington, East Yorkshire

From Bridlington, in summer you can take a boat trip along the coast to Bempton Cliffs to enjoy close views of the busy seabird colony there. Alternatively, visit in autumn to try the RSPB's 'Shearwater and Skua Cruise' –

a trip out to sea to look for migrating seabirds that are not usually seen close inshore. A supply of smelly 'chum' thrown from the boat ensures a constant escort of gulls, which are joined by Gannets, Fulmars, and with luck some rarer seabirds, such as Pomarine Skua and Balearic Shearwater.

Farne Islands, Northumberland

The Farnes are a cluster of small uninhabited islands, the nearest of them 2.5km from the mainland. They are home to mind-boggling numbers of nesting seabirds, and a trip there in summer is an extraordinary experience as you will be able to get extremely close to the birds. Access is strictly controlled but most trips allow a couple of hours on each of Staple Island

and Inner Farne. On Staple Island you will see Puffins, Guillemots, Razorbills, Shags, Eiders, Fulmars, Kittiwakes and various other gulls. Inner Farne has all of these and also a large colony of Arctic Terns – you will need to wear a hat to protect your head from their sharp bills as they launch dive-bombing attacks when you walk past their nests. Dolphins are sometimes seen from the crossing, and so are Gannets. For those who prefer undersea life, there are also diving trips to the Farnes, offering the chance to explore wrecks and have close encounters with seals.

WALES

Skomer Island, Pembrokeshire
Skomer and its neighbour Skokholm are both managed by the Welsh Wildlife Trust and are famous for their Manx Shearwater colonies. Skomer, the larger of the two islands, is home to about half the entire

Left The Farne Islands off Northumberland offer perhaps the best opportunity in Britain to watch Puffins at close range.

Below A visit to Skomer island in summer is a chance to really get away from it all and have some unforgettable wildlife encounters.

world population of the species. It also has some 10,000 breeding pairs of Puffins as well as other seabirds, and a unique mammal, the Skomer Vole, a subspecies of the Bank Vole. It is possible to arrange short stays on both Skomer and Skokholm, allowing you to experience the full magic of the shearwater colony as the birds fly ashore at dusk.

Grassholm Island, Pembrokeshire

Despite its name, this small island is more white than green in summer when nearly 40,000 pairs of Gannets arrive at their nest sites. The island is one of the RSPB's oldest nature reserves and is of global importance for its Gannets – it holds the third largest colony in the UK, and around 10 per cent of the total world Gannet population. Boats do not land on Grassholm but you can enjoy amazing views from boat trips, some of which also visit Ramsey Island, another RSPB reserve. From the boat you will see many other seabird species and possibly Harbour Porpoises and dolphins.

SCOTLAND

Isle of May, East Lothian

Lying in the mouth of the Firth of Forth, the 1.8km long Isle of May is an NNR, protected for its large seabird colonies. It is also an SPA and SAC. Puffins are the big draw for visitors but there are also good numbers of Kittiwakes, Guillemots, Razorbills and other cliff-face seabirds, with variable numbers of Common and Arctic Terns nesting on the flat areas.

Right Grassholm island off Pembrokeshire is 'Gannet central'.

Below Mousa's famous broch provides homes for numerous pairs of nesting Storm Petrels.

Cetaceans and seals are often seen from the island and from the boat crossing. The famous Bass Rock (page 190), a small volcanic island which holds the largest colony of Gannets in the world, is also in the Firth of Forth, and there are many options for boat trips that take you close to the island.

Mousa, Shetland

A small island off the south-eastern coast of Mainland, Mousa is famous for its European Storm-petrels, which nest in an abandoned broch (Iron Age drystone tower), but also on the boulder beaches that fringe the island. Boulder beaches, made of rocks up to 1 metre across, are less stable than solid rock shores but offer far more in the way of cracks and nooks, into which these small seabirds can squeeze but larger predators can't follow. The rocks also offer moorings for seaweeds and molluscs, while the flat beaches hold some 200 moulting Common Seals each August. Offshore, other seabirds including Arctic Terns and Arctic Skuas can be seen, and from the ferry crossing you could see Harbour Porpoises.

Boat trips from Gairloch, Highland

The north-west coast of the highlands is prime whale-watching country, and from any headland overlooking the Atlantic you could easily see dolphins or a Minke Whale. Board a boat for an even better chance of encounters. Species seen have included rare species such as Sei Whale, Long-finned Pilot Whale and Northern Bottlenose Whale, plus Risso's Dolphin, in addition to the commoner cetaceans. You should also see seabirds including Great and Arctic Skuas.

Fair Isle, Shetland

The most remote inhabited UK island, Fair Isle lies in between Shetland and Orkney, the nearest point being Sumburgh Head on Shetland Mainland, 39km away. It belongs to the National Trust for Scotland, and is home to one of the most important bird observatories in Britain. About 70 people live permanently on the island, and most of the supplies they need arrive by boat. Because of the time it takes to get here, most visitors arrange to stay for at least a

Far left Every available square inch of horizontal rock ledge is used by nesting seabirds on Rathlin island.

Left A boat trip to Puffin island off County Kerry should provide close views of Manx Shearwaters.

week, often at the observatory. The island is best known for its track record of very rare migrant birds, but it also has an important breeding seabird population, with both Arctic and Great Skuas and large numbers of Puffins and Arctic Terns.

IRELAND

Rathlin Island, Co Antrim

This hook-shaped, 6km-long island with a human population of around 1000 holds the most important seabird colony in Northern Ireland with tens of thousands of seabirds, including all the usual cliff-face nesting birds. The RSPB runs a seabird centre here with CCTV giving point-blank views of nesting birds, and you can see them with your own eyes from the trails. Careful management has encouraged Choughs to return here after 20 years of absence, and from the island and the ferry crossing from Ballycastle there is also a chance of seeing cetaceans.

Puffin Island, Co Kerry

A small island managed by Birdwatch Ireland, it can be visited for day trips by boat from the larger, inhabited island of Valentia. It holds important colonies of Manx Shearwaters and European Storm-petrels, as well as up to 10,000 Puffins and other commoner seabirds.

INDEX

ACKNOWLEDGMENTS

Firstly, I would like to thank Lisa Thomas for commissioning this book, and for patiently and thoughtfully nurturing its development from idea to finished work. I'd also like to thank the rest of the Bloomsbury team for backing the project and Nicola Liddiard for the lovely page layout.

The beauty of our coastline and the special magic of coastal wildlife-watching has inspired me ever since childhood, thanks to a seaside upbringing. I must thank my mother, Anne Taylor, and my father, Laurence Taylor, who encouraged me in my passion for wildlife from before I can remember. They gave me enough freedom to safely explore land, shore and sea close to home, and made it possible for me to visit and get to know wonderful wild coastal places further afield. My lovely sister Alison was a constant companion through those childhood summers at the seaside, and I hope in years to come we'll enjoy more days like those, even though the ice-cream is a lot more expensive now.

Over the years I have explored a multitude of wild and not so wild places around the coast of much of Britain, though there is of course much more that I've yet to discover. I would like to thank all the friends who've joined me on those adventures, and I hope you're all up for more of the same in the future.

PHOTO CREDITS

Pictures by Marianne Taylor except as below:

Shutterstock: 3 Helen Hotson; 5 Elle1; 6 Michael Thaler; 7 Matt Train; 8 Paul Cowan; 9 Paul Reeves Photography; 10 Ken C Moore; 13 Mike Charles; 15 Matt Gibson; 16 Yury Smelov; 19 Atosan; 27 Menno Schaefer; 29t Ronald Wilfred Jansen; 29b Hugh Lansdown; 32l Martin Fowler; 32r Giedriius; 33 Budimir Jevtic; 34 Stephen Rees; 39tl David Young; 39br Erni; 40r Andrea Fiore; 40b Wolfgang Kruck; 41t Spumador; 42 Wil Tilroe-Otte; 45 Ian Woolcock; 51 Creative Nature Media; 52 Menno Schaefer; 55 Vladislav T. Jirousek; 57 Moore Designs; 59 Bildagentur Zoonar GmbH; 62 Gordon Bell; 63 Pitamaha; 65b Siim Sepp; 66 Tony Carr; 67b Siim Sepp; 69 Erni; 71 Marcel Clemens; 72t Alexander Erdbeer; 72b Erni; 74 Erni; 74b Efiplus; 79c Robert L Kothenbeutel; 80 Will Iredale; 81b Andrew Roland; 82c Chris Moody; 82b Max Lindenthaler; 84l ; 84r Boonchuay Promjiam; 86 Matteo Photos; 87t Kevin Eaves; 87b 1_Weblogiq; 88 Erni; 89 Nicholas Peter Gavin Davies; 90t CLS Design; 90b Mark Caunt; 91 Bildagentur Zoonar GmbH; 96 Menno Schaefer; 100 TT Photo; 103t Wolverine1023; 103b Arno van Dulmen; 104r Wolfgang Kruck; 111t Jason Salmon; 111b Mark Caunt; 113r Roger Meerts; 115r Bildagentur Zoonar GmbH; 116 Erni; 121t Mirna; 121b Gertjan Hooijer; 122b Lynsey Allan; 123t David P Stephens; 123b MP cz; 125 Joingate; 126 Andrew Roland; 129 Andreas Altenburger; 131 Andy Fox Photography; 132t Martin Fowler; 132bl Jo Ann Snover; 135b David Dohnal; 136 Allou; 138t Nick Hawkes; 138b Martin Fowler; 139 V. Belov; 140l Wolfgang Kruck; 140r Chris Moody; 144t ; 144b ; 151r raulbaenacasado; 156 Daniel J. Rao; 158 KOO; 159t Amanda Hsu; 159b Vitaly Ilyasov; 160 David Hughes; 162 Neil Mitchell; 163r salpics32; 163b Gail Johnson; 164 Gail Johnson; 166t Erni; 166b Bill Spiers; 169 MV Photo; 170 Kevin Eaves; 172b Paul J Martin; 173t Ian Woolcock; 173b Ron Ellis; 177 Ian Woolcock; 179 Erni; 180 Shahid Ali Khan; 183 Erni; 184 Steve Byland; 185 fiddlemily; 186 Sergejus Lamanosovas; 187 Georgios Alexandris; 188 Spumador; 190 Hector Ruiz Villar; 192 TT Photo; 194t Colette3; 197 Maisna; 198t Marten House; 198b Wolfgang Kruck; 199b Mike Charles; 200t Em-Jott; 200b TT Photo; 202 PHB.cz (Richard Semik).
Getty Images: 78 Peter Macdiarmid / Staff.
FLPA: 176t Mike Lane/FLPA; 182 Imagebroker/FLPA; 195t Mammal Fund Earthviews/FLPA; 203 David Tipling/FLPA.
Nature Picture Library: 195b Mark Carwardine/NPL.